Serbia

Serbia

Revised Edition

BY JOANN MILIVOJEVIC

Enchantment of the World
Second Series

Children's Press®

A Division of Scholastic Inc.

NEW YORK   TORONTO   LONDON   AUCKLAND   SYDNEY
MEXICO CITY   NEW DELHI   HONG KONG
DANBURY, CONNECTICUT

Frontispiece: Serbian children in traditional dress

Consultant: Tatyana Nesterova, Undergraduate International Studies Program,
  The Ohio State University, Columbus

Please note: All statistics are as up-to-date as possible at the time of publication.

Book production by Herman Adler Design

Library of Congress Cataloging-in-Publication Data

Milivojevic, JoAnn.
      Serbia / JoAnn Milivojevic. – Rev. ed.
        p. cm. – (Enchantment of the world. Second series)
Includes bibliographical references and index.
 ISBN 0-516-22695-9
1. Serbia. I. Title. II. Series
 DR1940 .M55 2003
 949.71—dc21

                                    2002008262

Acknowledgments

I'd like to thank my mother, Radmila Milivojevic, who has fostered relationships between me and my relatives in Serbia. Special thanks to Mira and Sasa Obradovic for their research assistance.

Cover photo:
Studenica
Monastery

Contents

Priština

Traditional dress

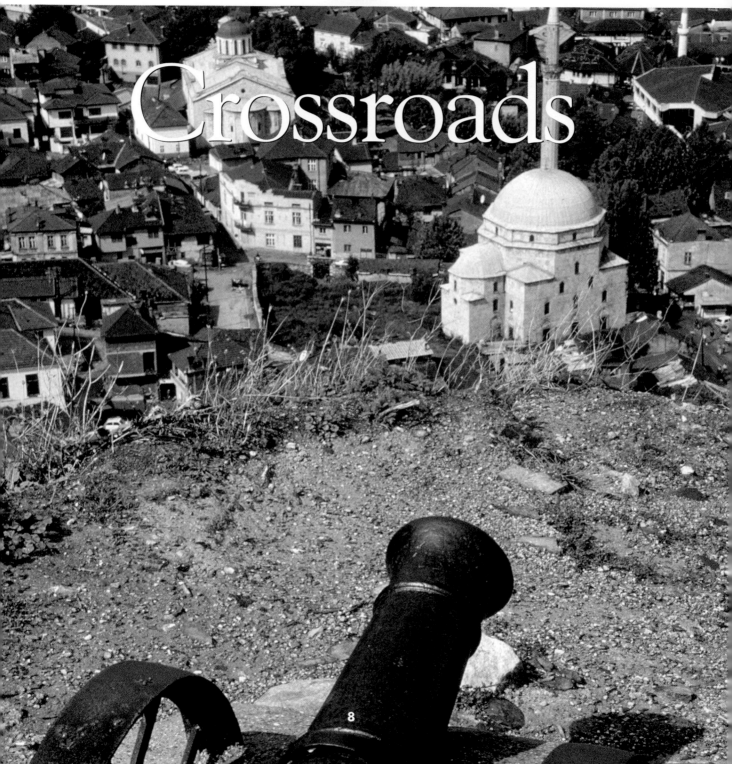

Crossroads

S ERBIA IS A LAND OF MEDIEVAL MONASTERIES, INTRICATE mosaics, and epic poems. Many artists, scholars, inventors, and politicians, including Ivo Andrić, winner of the 1961 Nobel prize for literature, and Nikola Tesla, the electrical engineer who discovered alternating current (AC) are of Serbian descent. Serbia is more than 800 years old. To understand Serbia's history, it is useful to examine its culture, religion, art, economy, and politics.

Opposite: **A discarded canon near a mosque and an Orthodox church in Prizren, Kosovo**

The monastery of Peć

Many monasteries in Serbia are decorated with frescoes.

Centuries ago, Serbia stood wedged between two warring empires: the Ottoman in the south, and the Habsburg in the north. For many years these empires waged war on Serbian soil. The conflicts pitched people from many religious and political backgrounds against one another—and as time passed, these people all contributed to Serbia's culture. Today, Islamic mosques stand near Orthodox churches, ancient fresco paintings mingle with modern art, and Turkish coffee is served with *šljivovica*, a Serbian brandy.

Serbia may seem to be a world away from us, but in its crowded modern cities and quiet villages, the daily activities of its people will seem familiar. Serbs pick medicinal herbs for natural healing, wash down fast food with mineral water, surf the Internet, talk on cell phones, and listen to music with rock-and-roll roots, just as people do in many Western and other cultures.

The Balkans

The Balkans is a region of republics and countries that include Slovenia, Croatia, Bosnia and Herzegovina, Macedonia, Yugoslavia (divided into Serbia and Montenegro), Albania, Greece, Romania, Bulgaria, and Turkey. From the fourteenth to the nineteenth centuries, the Ottoman, or Turkish, Empire ruled much of this area. The word *balkan* means "mountain" in Turkish. It also is the name of a mountain range in Bulgaria and Serbia.

A Belgrade street scene

Living at a Crossroads

If you've done any cloud watching, you know that the fluffy white masses can take on familiar shapes. Similarly, the geographic outlines of countries can also resemble objects. Italy, for example, looks like a boot, with its heel near southern Yugoslavia.

As you look at a map of Serbia, you may notice that the northern part looks like the head of a lion. The animal's nose touches the borders of Hungary and Croatia. The Danube River curling east toward Novi Sad is the lion's open mouth. Under its chin is the border of Bosnia and Herzegovina. Its extended front legs are in Montenegro. Belgrade, where the lion's mane would be, is the capital city of both Serbia and Yugoslavia.

In 1918, several regions—Slovenia, Croatia, Bosnia and Herzegovina, Serbia, Macedonia, and Montenegro—joined to form the Kingdom of the Serbs, Croats, and Slovenes. The kingdom was renamed Yugoslavia in 1929. In the early 1990s, this union fell apart when several republics declared independence and broke away from Yugoslavia.

Geopolitical map of Serbia

SERBIA
- Cities of over 100,000 people
- Smaller cities and towns

0   50 miles
0   75 kilometers

HUNGARY

ROMANIA

CROATIA

BOSNIA AND HERZE- GOVINA

MONTENEGRO

ALBANIA

MACEDONIA

BULGARIA

Serbia

Danube R.

Tisa R.

Subotica

Sombor

Vojvodina

Zrenjanin

Novi Sad

Kruševdol Monastery

Belgrade

Pančevo

Šabac

Smederevo

Golubac fortress

Djerdap (Iron Gate)

Kučevo

Lepinski Vir

Arandjelovac

Valjevo

Topola

Central Serbia

Kragujevac

Zaječar

Čačak

Kraljevo

Morava R.

Danube R.

Monastery of Studencia

Žiča Monastery

Vrnjačka Banja

Kruševac

Raška

Niš

Dimitrovgrad

Leskovac

Kosovska Mitrovica

Patriciate of Peć

Peć

Priština

Novo Brdo

Kosovo

Gracanica Monastery

Djakovica

Uroševac

Prizren

Adriatic Sea

N
W   E
S

Today, the Federal Republic of Yugoslavia (FRY) consists of Serbia and Montenegro. Montenegro is a rocky and dry expanse that touches the Adriatic Sea north of Albania. Montenegrins and Serbs share a common cultural heritage.

Serbia is a gateway between central Europe and southern European countries such as Romania and Bulgaria. The Danube River, which flows through Serbia, provides an easy route for merchant ships to drop off and pick up goods. Serbia is not only a major trade area, however. It is a religious crossroads, where different beliefs exist. Most Serbs follow the Eastern Orthodox religion, but others practice Roman Catholicism or Islam.

Serbia is no stranger to conflict. Families were torn apart by the civil war of the early 1990s and the collapse of the country's economy, which left many without money and jobs. Just when the situation was improving, another deadly political conflict erupted in Kosovo, and it plunged Serbia into a bitter war. Many people lost their homes—and even their lives.

Serbs are a strong-willed and determined people. Today's government leaders are working hard to improve the country's economy. No matter what kind of political group is in power, Serbia's rich farmland will always be able to feed its people. In that respect, Serbs are fortunate.

Serbs at a Belgrade coffee bar opposite the National Television studios destroyed in the civil war.

Farmers driving a horse and wagon

From the Mountains to the Valleys

S ERBIA IS A LAND OF RUSHING RIVERS, DENSE FORESTS, damp caves, and mineral-rich mountains. Serbia measures 34,115 square miles (88,358 square kilometers), about the size of the U.S. state of Maine.

Flat plains stretch across the northernmost region of Serbia. The rest of the country is covered with rolling hills, green valleys, and high mountains. The Dinaric Alps are in the west, the Albanian Alps and the Šar Mountains rise in the southwest, and the Balkan Mountains lie in the southeast. The North Albanian Alps in southern Serbia have the nation's highest peaks, rising 8,714 feet (2,656 meters).

Many of Serbia's mountains, including the Kopaonik range, Tara, and Zlatibor, have become popular tourist centers. The mountainsides are covered with deciduous and evergreen forests, wildflower meadows, and grassy pastures. People flock to these areas to ski, fish, hike, and ride horses.

Opposite: **A mountain stream near Peć**

Hikers in a forest in eastern Serbia

A Land of Threes

Serbia can be divided into three geographical regions. In the north is the province of Vojvodina (VOY-voh-dee-na), a large area of fertile plains drained by the Danube, the Sava, and the Tisa Rivers. Central Serbia is a hilly area with the largest population of the three regions. In the south is the province of Kosovo, a drier and more rocky, mountainous region than Central Serbia.

Vojvodina

The name *Vojvodina* comes from the Serbian word *vojvoda*, which means "chieftain" or "duke." The area is an extension of the Great Hungarian Plain. Millions of years ago, this region was under the sea. Earthquakes eventually pushed the land above the water level. The province has three distinct sections: Srem, immediately north of the city of Belgrade; Bačka, in the northwest; and Banat, in the northeast.

Farmland in Vojvodina

Serbia's Geographical Features

Area: 34,115 square miles (88,358 sq km)

Largest City: Belgrade, population 1,602,226

Highest Mountain Peak: Daravica, 8,714 feet (2,656 m)

Longest Navigable River: The Danube travels for 365 miles (588 km) through Serbia.

Average Temperatures: 70°F (21°C) in July; 32°F (0°C) in January

Average Annual Rainfall: 25–35 inches (64–89 cm)

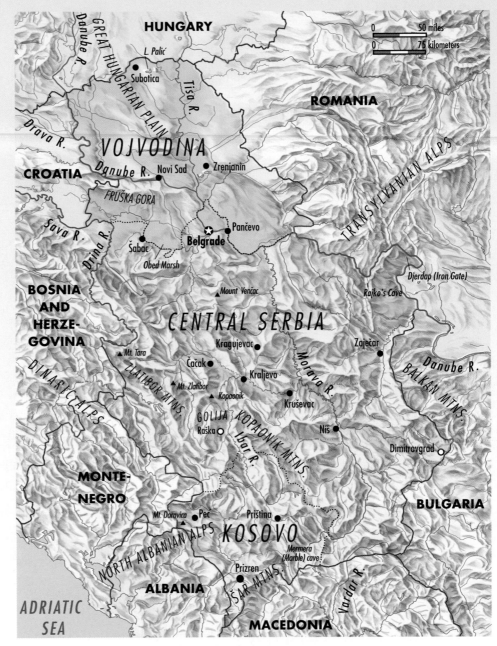

HUNGARY

ROMANIA

CROATIA

Drava R.

Danube R.

GREAT HUNGARIAN PLAIN

L. Palić

Subotica

Tisa R.

VOJVODINA

Novi Sad

Zrenjanin

FRUŠKA GORA

Sava R.

Drina R.

Belgrade

Pančevo

Šabac

Obed Marsh

TRANSYLVANIAN ALPS

Mount Venčac

Djerdap (Iron Gate)

Rajko's Cave

BOSNIA AND HERZE-GOVINA

CENTRAL SERBIA

Kragujevac

Zaječar

Danube R.

Mt. Tara

ZLATIBOR MTNS.

Čačak

Kraljevo

Morava R.

DINARIC ALPS

Mt. Zlatibor

Kopaonik

Kruševac

BALKAN MTNS.

GOLIJA

Raška

Ibar R.

KOPAONIK MTNS.

Niš

Dimitrovgrad

MONTE-NEGRO

Mt. Daravica

Peć

Priština

KOSOVO

Mermera (Marble) cave

BULGARIA

NORTH ALBANIAN ALPS

Prizren

ŠAR MTNS.

Vardar R.

ADRIATIC SEA

ALBANIA

MACEDONIA

0   50 miles
0   75 kilometers

A mountaintop view of
Fruška Gora

Unlike most of Vojvodina, parts of Srem have gentle, rolling hills, including a low mountain range called Fruška Gora (FRU-shka Gohr-rah), which means "mountain of fruits." These mountains run between the marshy valleys of the Danube and the Sava Rivers. The hills rise to about 1,772 feet (540 m) and are capped with dense, deciduous forests. Much of the area is a national park protected by the government. Fruška Gora has more linden trees than anywhere else in Europe. It also has about 700 different kinds of herbs, many of which are used for medicine.

The Fragrant Linden

Linden trees are a favorite and useful tree in Serbia. Some grow as high as 80 feet (24 m). In springtime, the sweet scent of their small, white flowers fills the air. Bees make honey from the flowers. People put the petals to good use, too. They dry them to make tea and a special hair rinse. The tea is said to be effective for relieving colds, while the rinse adds shine and golden highlights to hair.

Farmers harvest many crops from the rich and fertile land in Srem; especially popular are grapes. Other fruits that grow here include plums, pears, and apples. People enjoy fresh fruits or make them into delicious jams called *slatko*. The wine from this region, *fruškogorski biser*, is famous throughout Serbia. Serbia exports some wine and other fruit products, although many families produce their own to use at home.

People who are born in Fruška Gora tend to stay there. Farms and vineyards have been passed down through many generations. It is not unusual for a Fruška Gora family to have lived there for 300 years.

A bountiful harvest of grapes will produce wine for this family in Srem.

Krušedol Monastery

Krušedol Monastery is the largest and most important religious building in Fruška Gora. Constructed in 1516 in the Serbian-Byzantine style, it contains frescoes depicting sixteenth-century political and religious leaders. Krušedol contains the tombs of Serbian royalty, including that of King Milan Obrenović, who died in 1901.

The Obed Marsh is a large wetland found in Srem.

In addition to being an agricultural zone, the Fruška Gora range is historically important. In the late 1300s, the Ottoman Turks invaded southern Serbia. Many people fled there for this region, where the mountains create a natural fortress overlooking the plains. From the tops of the mountains, Serbs could see intruders approaching miles away.

Fruška Gora is home to eighteen monasteries, some dating from the fourteenth century. In those days, churches were not only religious institutions, they were also schools for general studies as well as cultural arts centers. Painting and literature flourished in them. As villages grew, more monasteries were built.

Today, residents of Belgrade often spend their weekends in Fruška Gora, staying in one of the pretty white stucco cottages dotting the countryside. About an hour's drive from the Belgrade city limits, Fruška Gora's fresh air and forest greenery provide a welcome relief from the city.

Srem is also home to the vast Obed Marsh. A marsh is a very wet, treeless region along the edge of a river. The Obed Marsh was created by the floodwaters of the Sava and the Danube Rivers. More than 200 species of birds dwell in the tall grasses of Obed Marsh, where they nest and seek food. Other marsh wildlife includes exotic wildflowers and a variety of grasses, such as cattails and rushes (grasses with hollow stems). This wet world also hosts frogs and water bugs, including a species that skates on the surface the water.

Bačka

The flat and fertile region known as Bačka (BOTCH-ka) is the agricultural heart of Serbia. If you were to view Bačka from above, you'd see neat squares of green, yellow, and brown. That's the handiwork of farmers who carefully plant corn, maize (a certain type of corn), wheat, barley, and other crops in square plots. Produce from Bačka is sold in Subotica (SUE-bow-tee-tza), the central marketplace and northern-most city in Serbia.

An endless field of sunflowers in Bačka

The haystack on this farm took days to build and will provide food for the farm's livestock.

Throughout the year, tall mounds of hay dot Bačka's land-scape. Haystacks are a method of storing hay. Farmers pull hay from the stacks to feed livestock. Building a haystack is hard work. Each requires two people and takes several days to create. Workers place a layer of hay around a wooden post and stomp on the hay to flatten it. They keep adding layers and flattening them until the haystack is at least 10 feet (3 m) high.

Lake Palić in Subotica is a popular resort area. Visitors take relaxing nature walks in the pretty parks filled with flower gardens and sculptures. For more rigorous exercise, some people play tennis on one of the many nearby courts, while watersports enthusiasts might fish, swim, water-ski, or look for the Lake Palić monster.

Local legend says that in the depths of Lake Palić lives a monster much like the famed "Nessie" of Scotland's Loch Ness. Lake Palić's monster is called the *Palićka Neman* (PAH-leech-ka NEH-mahn). The legendary monster is said to be more than 20 feet (6 m) long, with a very long tail. Few people claim to have actually seen it. Those who have report that they didn't get a clear look because the tricky Neman only surfaces during misty weather.

A Serbian Patriot

The city of Subotica was founded in the sixteenth century by Duke Subota Vrlic, during the reign of Tsar Jovan Nenad (tsars were Eastern European emperors). Tsar Nenad became a local hero when he led a small army of Serbian patriots against a Turkish invasion.

Subotica's Lake Palić

Banat

Also within the province of Vojvodina is Banat (BAA-not), which borders Romania. Vast plains and marshy valleys make up much of its landscape. In the southeast sand deposits form picturesque dunes called *deliblato* (DAY-LEE-blah-toe). Banat is from the Romanian word *ban*, meaning ruler.

Central Serbia

Šumadija is a forested central region in Serbia. The word *šuma* (SHOO-ma) means "forest." In the east, the Balkan Mountains form Serbia's border with Bulgaria and Romania, with peaks as high as 6,000 feet (1,828 m).

Šumadija is well known for its corn, wheat, hay, mineral water, goose and duck down for jackets, and pork and beef products. It is also the site of Mount Venčac, where beautiful white marble is mined.

Every year in the town of Arandjelovac, a Marble and Sound festival is held for two weeks during the summer. The town becomes alive with musical concerts and sculpture contests, all free to the public. Artists from all over Serbia chisel the glistening local white rock to create fabulous forms. Since the festival has been running for more than thirty years, the countryside is decorated with many of these beautiful sculptures. The white statues become part of a permanent outdoor exhibit. The town is also famous for Knez Miloš, a manufacturing plant that bottles naturally fizzy mineral water, which is sold locally and internationally.

Serbia is filled with large lakes, flowing rivers, cold mountain streams, and natural hot springs. The Danube, the republic's most important river, has three main tributaries: the Sava, the Tisa, and the Morava Rivers. Before it branches off into those tributaries, the Danube River starts its long journey in Germany's Black Forest region, flows east, and finally empties into the Black Sea off the coast of Romania.

The Danube is the second-longest river in Europe (about 1,700 miles, or 2,736 km) and it is the only major European river to flow from west to east. This vital waterway links central Europe with Eastern Europe. Its longest navigable portion, 365 miles (588 km), lies within Serbia, making the country part of a valuable trade route. Merchant marines guide their ships along the Danube and its tributaries and transfer their goods at shipping ports in Belgrade, Novi Sad, Pančevo, and Smederevo.

Belgrade's location on two rivers makes it an important shipping port.

Iron Gate Gorge

Djerdap (JER-dahp) National Park has a gorge known as the Iron Gate. The steep, rocky walls of the Iron Gate Gorge rise about 984 feet (300 m). The Iron Gate is Europe's longest gorge, at 62 miles (100 km). Rivers erode rock and leave behind gorges. This may take thousands—or sometimes millions—of years. The Danube wore away this rock, leaving behind tall, sheer cliffs. Here, the Danube plunges 330 feet (101 m), in one of the deepest riverbeds in the world.

Engineers created a dam to harness the power of this mighty river for electricity. The Djerdap hydroelectric power plant (right) is one of Europe's largest. It produces electricity not only for Yugoslavia but also for neighboring European countries, who purchase the power.

Natural Healing

Serbia has more than 140 mineral springs and 53 spas. The spas are health centers, and they are the oldest tourist resorts in Serbia. They use the earth's natural springs to heal a variety of ailments. Vrnjačka Banja, for instance, has three mineral-water springs, one containing warm water and two with cold water. Doctors prescribe spa waters to remedy stomach problems, liver and kidney disorders, and heart conditions. The prescriptions require patients to soak in, sip, or wash with particular mineral waters.

Some of Serbia's springs have been in use since ancient Roman times, when nobles and heads of state visited them. Today they are widely used by the general population.

The southernmost region of Serbia is considered the cradle of Serbian culture. Here, in Kosovo, the first Serbian state began to expand in the twelfth century.

Kosovo's rocky soil is not suited for planting, but farmers manage to coax a few crops to grow—mostly maize and rye. Some of the rocks contain valuable minerals such as silver, lead, and zinc. The minerals are mined and exported. Local residents also raise sheep and goats, grazing them on the area's hillsides.

Sheep graze on a Kosovo hillside.

Looking at Serbia's Cities

Novi Sad (population 179,626) sits on the Danube River in Vojvodina Province. Local factories manufacture porcelain, soap, and textiles. Important local sites include Petrovaradin's Fortress, which dates to ancient Roman times, the Serbian National Theater, and a university. Founded in the seventeenth century, Novi Sad was part of Hungary until the Kingdom of the Serbs, Croats, and Slovenes was formed in 1918.

Priština (top) (population 108,083), the capital of Kosovo Province, is near the Kopaonik Mountains. It was the capital of the Serbian Empire before the Ottoman Turks' victory at the Battle of Kosovo. A fourteenth-century monastery, Gracanica, is nearby. The Museum of Kosovo-Metohija and a university are also in Priština.

Subotica (right) (population 100,386), the northernmost city in Serbia, is an important commercial, agricultural, and intellectual center. Agricultural products are processed, packaged, and sold there. Subotica borders Hungary, so the local music, architecture, food, and people often have Hungarian origins. The Hungarian language also appears on street signs and in newspapers and books in the region.

What Do I Wear Today?

The weather in Serbia is similar to that of the midwestern United States, although it is generally less humid. Serbia has what is called a "continental" climate: Its winters are very cold and its summers are warm. In winter, you need a heavy coat, a hat, mittens or gloves, and a scarf, especially in the northern areas of the country. If you like snow, you'll find plenty of it in the mountains of central Serbia. In southern Kosovo, however, the weather is somewhat milder.

Serbia's summers are warm and pleasant, reaching highs of about 80° Fahrenheit (27° Celsius). It is drier and hotter the farther south you go. On the whole, the mountain regions have cooler, shorter summers and more severe winters than the lower areas of Serbia.

This family is well bundled up for a winter sleigh ride.

Where the Wild Things Grow

M UCH OF SERBIA'S LAND IS
fertile. The forests and valleys are a
haven for wild plants and animals.
Serbian farmers grow a variety of crops including grapes, wheat,
and corn, and the many forests provide timber for industry.

Among the many kinds of trees that grow in Serbia is the
oak, with rounded leaves that turn gold and red in the fall.
Serbia also has many evergreens. Serbs harvest the sap from
evergreen trees to make a spicy-sweet incense. Serbia's forests
are home to deer, foxes, wolves, wild boars, bears, stags, wild
lynx, and martens (squirrel-like animals with a long bushy tail
and a silky brown coat). Forest birds include grouse, partridges, swallows, nightingales, and woodpeckers.

**A pine marten
leaves through the forest.**

Left: **A wild boar with young**

Right: **A red fox**

Opposite: **The forests of
Serbia are abundant with
plant and animal life.**

Where the Wild Things Grow **31**

How Incense Is Made

Some incense is made from tree sap. Pine trees produce resin, a thick, brownish substance that oozes out of the tree. In Serbia, people make their own incense by scraping the sap off pine trees. The sticky mass is rolled out into a pencil shape and then pinched into small, pill-sized chunks. The pieces are sprinkled with cornstarch and left to air-dry. Sometimes scented oils are poured into the sap before it is rolled out. People burn the incense in small trays called *censers*. Today, Serbian church incense is often made by monks.

Serbia has so many farms that it has been called the "Garden of the Balkans." Vegetables and fruit flourish in its rich soil. Sweet red strawberries appear earliest in the growing season. Next come cherries and raspberries, peaches, apricots, and blackberries. However, no summer in Serbia would be complete without delicious melons. When summer gives way to fall, grapes, apples, and pears are abundant.

One fruit is honored above all the rest—the plum. It is Serbia's national fruit. Plum jam and plum brandy (šljvovica) are manufactured in Serbia and enjoyed around the world.

Fungus Among Us

Mushroom lovers find plenty of their favorite fungi underneath the pine trees of Serbia. The mountains of Serbia provide the perfect mushroom-growing climate for varieties from frilly pink mushrooms to honeycombed morel mushrooms. Visitors rely on skilled guides for mushroom-picking expeditions, however, because some mushrooms are poisonous.

Lilacs Fit for a Queen

In the twelfth century, King Uros Nemanja married a woman from France. To make her feel welcome, he planted lilac bushes to remind her of her homeland. The lilacs took root and flourished along the fertile banks of the Ibar River. Their sweet fragrance graces the country air to this day.

There's plenty of mooing, cackling, and snorting going on in Serbia. Cows, chickens, and pigs are the most common farm animals. A farmer's whole family helps care for the farm's animals. They attach bells to their livestock so they can find a stray who has wandered from the herd. You can hear the softly clanging bells around the countryside.

Herds of sheep are a common sight in Serbia.

In Serbian villages, called *selos* (SELL-ohs), many old customs still thrive. Older village women usually wear traditional peasant garb—a long black skirt, a plain blouse, and a head scarf. You might see one of these women with a herd of animals, carrying an ax slung over her shoulder. She uses the ax to chop tree branches for goats and sheep, which love to munch on the leafy twigs.

National Symbol

The ancient national symbol of Serbia is the double-headed white eagle. It originated during the Nemanja Dynasty, named after the royal family who expanded Serbian territory in the twelfth century. The symbol, an image of the mythical king of animals, appears on Serbia's coat of arms (left).

Serbs keep and care for pets such as dogs, cats, and fish. In the country, dogs and cats are rarely allowed inside homes. Instead, they sleep outside. They are often given jobs such as herding sheep and chasing away mice.

There are many dog breeds in Serbia. A popular breed in both city and country is the little Pekinese. Other favorites include dalmatians (originally from the former Yugoslav republic of Dalmatia), rottweilers, German shepherds, huskies, and mixed breeds. All dogs in Serbia must have yearly shots. Instead of wearing tags to indicate inoculations, they are tattooed with the information on the inside of one ear.

Pekinese are a popular breed of dog in Serbia.

Belgrade Zoo

When you think of a zoo, you usually think of animals such as lions, elephants, and ostriches. The Belgrade Zoo, also called the Good Hope Garden, certainly has all of these, but it also has a section for dogs. Here you can see the Sop, a Serbian defense dog that is a mixed breed of mastiff, Bosnian wolf, and terrier. These breeds were selected to produce a smart, fast, and strong dog. These dogs are specially trained for military and police jobs. The brown or black dogs have thick fur and weigh up to 130 pounds (59 kilograms).

Unlike the United States, where grassy lawns surround many private homes, in Serbia yards are filled with flowers like sweet-smelling hyacinths, climbing roses, and colorful tulips. Flowering linden and plum trees grow around many homes as well.

All those trees and flowers attract bees. Because bees cross-pollinate plants, many fruit growers keep them for that very purpose. In addition to helping fruit trees, bees produce honey. The flavor of the honey depends on the type of flowers the bees visit. Beekeepers construct wooden boxes into which busy bees dive to deposit nectar into honeycombs. The keepers extract the honey from the combs and store it in large jugs. You can see blue or white bee boxes not just in the country, but also in mid-sized towns.

This beekeeper keeps a close watch on the honey being made by his bees.

Rock of Ages

Rocks tell stories—if you know how to read their language. Fossils found in rocks are like geological history books. Scientists who study these rocks have discovered that millions of years ago, the entire Balkan region was a tropical garden, complete with palm trees. Evidence of this has been found in fossil spores from Fruška Gora south to Montenegro. Some fossil remains are 180 million to 200 million years old, making them part of the Old Jurassic Period—a time when dinosaurs roamed the earth.

Battlefield Flower

Serbia has no official national flower, but most of its citizens love the *božur*, or red peony. Legend has it that the flower was once white but it turned to red because of the blood shed during the Battle of Kosovo in 1389.

Caves and Karst

Karst (collapsed limestone) has created many underground caves and craters in Serbia. When limestone goes through metamorphosis, a rare phenomenon, it produces a beautiful marble. That's how the marble cliffs developed around the Mermerna (Marble) Cave near Priština. The cave's ceiling is covered with stalactites, which are icicle-shaped masses of calcium carbonate. The pillars are quite tall; some are 16 feet (5 m) high and have unusual spikes on them. The colors inside the cave range from white to red, with many shades in between.

When Serbia Began

THE EARLIEST SIGNS OF LIFE IN SERBIA HAVE BEEN FOUND in the Djerdap National Park, near the Danube River. In 1965, archaeologists dug beneath piles of sand and muck and found strange stone sculptures resembling fish-faced human forms. They dated these sculptures to 7000 B.C., in the Middle, or Mesolithic, Stone Age. The etched stones were the work of artisans from a settled community known as the Lepenski Vir culture.

Opposite: **Huts dot the hillside above the Danube River at Lepenski Vir, the oldest known settlement on the Danube.**

Rock scuptures at Lepenski Vir

Lepenski Vir is significant because it was a settled community at a time when most people in Europe were nomadic hunters who set up temporary shelters. Easy access to water, fish, and other wildlife that lived along the Danube River helped encourage settlement there.

Along with the mysterious sculptures, archaeologists at Lepenski Vir also unearthed jewelry, tools, and carved plaques with raised symbols that look like letters. The symbols are thought to be an early form of written communication—making this culture quite advanced for its time. Lepenski Vir is believed to be among the oldest Stone Age settlements in Europe. Artifacts from this ancient culture are on display at the National Museum in Belgrade.

Bogomils

The Bogomils were a religious and political group that thrived in the Balkans between the tenth and the fifteenth centuries. Bogomils were "ascetic dualists," meaning that they followed very strict rules, lived simple lives, and believed that there were two independent godlike beings, one good and one evil. They rejected the power of the established Christian church, preferring to follow their own beliefs. This photo is of a Bogomil cemetery.

Serbs and Slavs

Serbs are of Slavic descent, but there is some debate as to the origins of the Slavs. Did they migrate from the Carpathian Mountains, or did they come from the early settlements around the Danube River? No one knows for sure. We do know that some early Slavs were farmers and herders.

Beginning about A.D. 150, these Slavic tribes began to migrate. To the north, they followed the rivers through the forests of Russia. To the west, they met up with Germanic and Celtic tribes and occupied much of Central Europe. By the seventh century, Slavs had reached as far south as the Adriatic Sea.

Establishment of Serbia

The first Serbian kingdom emerged around the eleventh century. Serbs initially settled in the region of Kosovo called Raška. (Today this area is known by its Turkish name, Sandzak.) As the Serbian kingdom expanded, local leaders sought independence from outside rulers. To get a better understanding of what life was like then, we need an understanding of who held power and how Serbian communities were organized.

Balkans, 11th–15th Centuries

- Byzantine Empire, 1050
- Byzantine Empire, 1215
- Ottoman Empire, 1390
- Ottoman Empire, 1480

The Power Holders

The Balkan region was much like the middle of a giant chessboard, where players constantly moved around, trying to gain territory for their side. Before the first century A.D., the Roman Empire ruled much of southern Europe, including the Balkans. The Roman Empire eventually divided into two parts, east and west. In A.D. 330, Emperor Constantine established Constantinople in Asia Minor on the site of the ancient city of Byzantium. The eastern Roman Empire became known as the Byzantine Empire. Through time, the western portion of the Roman Empire grew weaker, while the Byzantine Empire grew stronger.

Peasants vow their allegiance and service to the king's vassal.

Feudalism—From Tribes to Kingdoms

Feudalism was a system of economic, political, and social organization structured like a pyramid, with a king (or other ruler), at the top, who owned all the land. The ruler handed parcels of land to vassals, who managed the land and the peasants who lived on it. The peasants farmed the land. In return, the peasants had to give the king (through a vassal) a percentage of everything the land produced: fruits, vegetables, honey, wine, and livestock such as sheep and pigs. Vassals, who also profited from the produce of the land, had to promise to be loyal to the king. This included serving in the king's army.

The feudal system developed around the eighth century because of the constant wars in the Balkans and Europe. It was a way to organize armies and keep people under the control of their rulers. What was all the fighting about? One of the main reasons was land ownership. Until the thirteenth century, land was the primary source of income. The more land a person had, the more crops and livestock that landowner could produce, sell, and exchange, becoming ever more powerful in the process. This power had its price, however. Other landowners would try to steal land to expand their own kingdoms. For this reason, military loyalty was vital to the feudal system. However, some loyalties didn't last long.

The Royal Family Nemanja Unifies Serbs

By the twelfth century Serbia was organized into various feudal states. The main Serbian principality was Raška (present-day Kosovo and parts of Bosnia). It was a dependency of the Byzantine Empire, as were other surrounding areas. The royal Nemanja family ruled Raška. Even though a prince or king ruled a particular area, he might still owe allegiance to someone with greater power. Such was the case in Raška until the Nemanjas challenged that arrangement.

Stefan Nemanja, born in Zeta (present-day Montenegro) was related to the ruling family in Zeta and Raška. He was baptized a Roman Catholic because at the time of his birth, the Roman Empire ruled Zeta. In 1168, Stefan Nemanja became grand *župan* (zhu-pan), or leader, of Raška.

In 1172, Nemanja was imprisoned by Byzantine emperor Manuel and was carried off to Constantinople. Nemanja would have been killed, but Manuel spared him. While in Constantinople, Nemanja fell in love with the Byzantine culture. After his release from prison, Nemanja returned to rule Raška, was rebaptized into the Byzantine faith, and became a devout Eastern Orthodox Christian.

Stefan Nemanja is important to Serbian history for two reasons. He united the local population by building a powerful kingdom, and he constructed magnificent Eastern Orthodox monasteries. Many rulers built churches and monasteries because it enhanced their power and status. The Nemanja monasteries, however, served a greater purpose for the Serbian people. When Serbia was occupied by the Ottoman Turks, these monasteries helped the Serbian people keep their faith and culture alive.

Brotherly Love, Brotherly Hatred

Stefan Nemanja had three sons: Rastko (better known by his religious name, Sava), Stefan, and Vukan. Sava became a monk and convinced his father to give up the throne to become a monk as well. At age eighty-two, the elder Nemanja did so, but instead of passing the throne to his eldest son, Vukan, as was the tradition, Nemanja gave it to his middle son, Stefan. He did so because Stefan married into a ruling Byzantine family. The elder Stefan believed that his middle son would have more power in the Byzantine emperor's court. Vukan was given rulership of properties elsewhere, but he was not pleased with the arrangement.

Nemanja Sainthood

After years of ruling Raška, Stefan Nemanja the elder and his wife retired and devoted their lives to the Eastern Orthodox Church. They joined their youngest son, Sava, at the "Holy Mountain," Mount Athos, in Greece. Mount Athos was the center of the Eastern Orthodox religion. The elder Nemanja later achieved sainthood as Saint Simeon. Sava was also made a saint. Today, there are churches named after Saint Simeon and Saint Sava.

Vukan aligned himself with the Roman Empire and waged war against his brother Stefan. In the meantime, the elder Stefan died. Sava brought his father's remains back to Serbia. The action helped establish peace between the warring brothers.

By this time, other wars were severely weakening the Byzantine Empire. In an effort to gain independence for Serbia, Sava asked the pope in Rome to bless Serbia and requested that the royal wreath be given to Stefan. It was done. Such a blessing was similar to receiving international recognition today. From that moment, Stefan became known as Stefan the First Crowned.

The Golden Age of Medieval Serbia

Beginning with Stefan the First Crowned, the Nemanja Dynasty ruled Serbia for the next 200 years. During this time, many aspects of Serbian life changed for the better. The country's territory expanded and great cities arose. Trade and commerce developed. The area's rivers became waterways for international trade. Serbs exported animals, cheese, furs, and honey. From the mountains, they extracted and exported gold, silver, and copper. They imported textiles, salt, and spices. Germany, Italy, and the Near East all traded with Serbia.

Serbia also became a recognized cultural and political force. Monasteries, especially in Kosovo, flourished as centers of Orthodox Christian teachings. The churches' architecture and frescoes (images made with watercolors painted onto wet plaster) are evidence of the kingdom's accomplishments. The "Golden Age" of Serbia is still a source of pride to many Serbs today.

Studenica

The Studenica Monastery complex, founded in the late twelfth century, is a home for monks to study, live, and pray. Because of its extraordinary artistic and cultural value, the complex is under the protection of UNESCO, an agency of the United Nations. This monastery is the largest and richest Orthodox monastery in Serbia.

The buildings in the complex are made of marble from the nearby hills. The windows and doorways are intricately carved. Inside are frescoes with text in Cyrillic, the alphabet of the Slavic language.

Golubac Fortress

Built in the fourteenth century on high cliffs over looking the Danube River, Golubac Fortress guards the entrance to the Iron Gate Gorge. The scene of many battles, Golubac is one of the finest medieval fortresses still standing in Serbia. A civilian settlement developed on a plateau in front of the fortress.

From Kingdom to Empire

The Serbian Empire eventually controlled most of what is now Yugoslavia (Serbia and Montenegro) and Albania, and it reached as far south as Greece. Stefan Dušan was the last great ruler of the Nemanja Dynasty. During his reign (1331–1355), Serbia had a mixed Serbian and Greek population. Dušan was tsar of the Serbs and Greeks, but this empire fell apart after his death.

While Serbia was gaining territory, however, the Ottoman Empire was also expanding. The Ottoman Turks came from central Asia. They were Muslims, followers of the teachings of Islam. Eventually the Ottoman Turks took over much of the Byzantine Empire's holdings. By the fourteenth century, the Ottoman Turks invaded Serbia, forever changing the course of its history.

The Fall of Serbia

On June 28, 1389, the Ottoman army was at Kosovo's gates demanding that the Serbs surrender. The Serbian forces were much smaller and would most certainly be crushed by the Turks. Serb military leader Prince Lazar Hrebeljanović could either surrender to the earthly kingdom, or sacrifice for the heavenly kingdom in the name of Christianity.

The battle that ensued took place at *Kosovo Polje*, which means "field of blackbirds." Lazar led his army into certain defeat. The battle devastated the Serbs, who lost most of their leaders. The area became a Turkish *pashalik*, or province. The defeat at Kosovo in 1389 is remembered in

"Tsartisa" Milica

After Prince Lazar was killed in battle, his wife, Milica, assumed power. She ruled until her son was old enough to take the throne. Milica cared for war widows, founded monasteries, and encouraged nuns to create intricate embroidered tapestries. Some of these tapestries hang in the National Museum in Belgrade.

Belgrade surrenders to the Ottomans.

epic folk songs passed down through generations of Serbs. Lazar was referred to as a *tsar* (emperor), although he was officially a prince.

The Ottomans spread farther into Serbian territory, seized the land, and enslaved the people. By 1459, the invasion of Serbia was complete. The Turks occupied Serbia for nearly 500 years, diminishing Serbia's economic, cultural, and civic development.

The Turks did allow Christians to keep their churches and monasteries. These institutions helped Serbs maintain their cultural and religious identity.

Independence Regained

The Serbs regained their independence in the nineteenth century, but only after more bloodshed. It took many battles to free themselves from the Turks. The pivotal battle, led by Miloš Obrenović in 1815, freed Serbia of Turkish domination. However, Serbia had lost most of the territory it once held. Obrenović became prince in 1817.

During the Russo-Turkish War of 1877–1878, Serbia and Russia joined to defeat Turkey in the Balkans. The 1878 Congress of Berlin returned Serbia's independence, but not all of its land. Austria took control of Bosnia and Herzegovina, where many Serbs lived. Serbia's relations with Austria became very tense.

As a result of the Congress of Berlin, the Ottoman Turks lost most of their European territory, Russian influence decreased in the Middle East, and Austria-Hungary and Great Britain grew more powerful. Neither the Balkan countries nor Russia were satisfied with what they received. This dissatisfaction was among the main causes of World War I (1914–1918).

In 1912, Serbs took an active part in the Balkan Wars, which gave them

Miloš Obrenović led the battle freeing Serbia of Turkish rule.

The Balkans, 1815–1877

Austrian Empire
Ottoman Empire

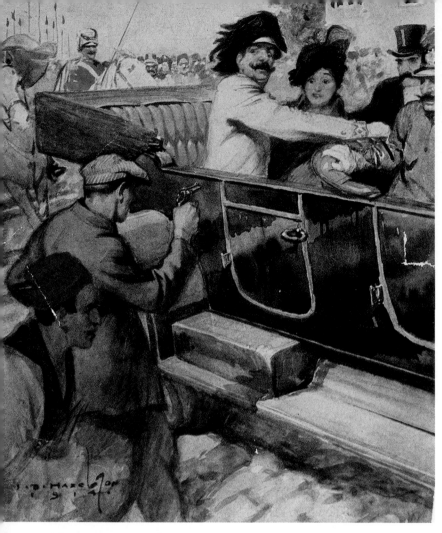

The assassination of Archduke Francis Ferdinand, from a painting by I. B. Hazelton

international recognition as well as territory in Macedonia and Kosovo, the cradle of their civilization. Serbia was becoming more powerful, and it made Austria-Hungary quite nervous.

World War I

In 1914, a Bosnian Serb nationalist named Gavrilo Princip assassinated the heir to the Austro-Hungarian throne, Archduke Francis Ferdinand, in Sarajevo, Bosnia. The Austro-Hungarian government held Serbia responsible, declared war, and invaded Serbia. By December, the country was occupied once again.

For the Serbs, independence had been hard won and was difficult to maintain. They were not alone; the Austro-Hungarian Empire also governed other Slavs. With these other Slavs, the Serbs grew determined to regain independence.

No Strength in Unity

When World War I ended in 1918, the leaders of Serbia, Croatia, Slovenia, Bosnia and Herzegovina, Macedonia, and

Assassination of a King

In October 1934, King Aleksandar of Yugoslavia traveled to Marseilles, France, to broaden the friendship between Yugoslavia and France. While there, he was assassinated by a member of the Ustasha, a Croatian extremist organization whose members opposed Aleksandar's policies. They wanted independence for Croatia. By murdering the forty-six-year-old king, they hoped to disorganize Yugoslavia and achieve independence. Citizens of both Serbia and Croatia were outraged by the act, however, and Yugoslavia remained intact until World War II (1939–1945). This photo was taken only minutes before Aleksandar's death.

Montenegro joined to become the Kingdom of the Serbs, Croats, and Slovenes. The country became Yugoslavia in 1929.

Yugoslavia united people of Slavic origin, but these groups had spent centuries under different governments and establishing different cultures. Disagreements arose over culture, religion, and government. The Slovenes and the Croatians were Roman Catholic, while the Serbs were Orthodox. In addition, after 500 years of Turkish rule, there were Turkish Muslims, and many Slavs had converted to Islam, so there was a sizable Muslim community as well. The idea of unity among these three groups of people seemed simple enough in theory, but it proved difficult in real life.

The leaders of the newly formed Yugoslavia couldn't agree on a form of government. Disagreement was especially strong between the Serbs and the Croatians. Serbs formed a large percentage of the Yugoslavian population and had once been independent. This tipped the balance of power in their favor. The government became a constitutional monarchy, led by Serbian king Aleksandar Karadjordjević. Belgrade became the capital of the new country.

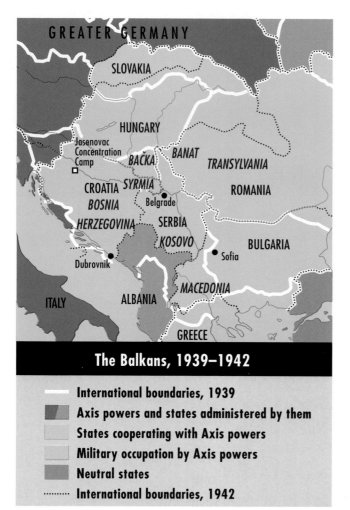

The Balkans, 1939–1942

— International boundaries, 1939

■ Axis powers and states administered by them

☐ States cooperating with Axis powers

☐ Military occupation by Axis powers

■ Neutral states

…… International boundaries, 1942

World War II

The main problem in Europe and the Balkans during World War II was the rise of the Fascist government in Italy and the National Socialist Party (Nazis) in Germany. In March 1941, Serbia closed its borders to keep

Germany from invading the Balkans. But this did not stop the Nazis—Adolf Hitler bombed Belgrade a month later.

The Germans also marched into Croatia, where they were considered liberators—troops that would free Croatia from Serbian dominance. The Yugoslav government fell apart, and people began to fight over who would be in charge. The stakes were high because the winner of the battle would rule the land. Serbia was pulled apart by both a civil war and a world war.

A Serbian Holocaust

Before World War II ended, a reign of terror as shocking as Hitler's murderous treatment of the Jews took place in Serbia. Between 1941 and 1945, about 750,000 Serbs, Jews, and Gypsies were murdered by a military and political regime called the Ustasha, led by Croatian nationalist Ante Pavelić.

When Yugoslavia collapsed in 1941, it was carved into pieces. The Germans occupied Serbia, while Pavelić ruled the new Independent State of Croatia (*Nezavisna Država Hrvatska*, or NDH), which essentially became a "puppet" state run by the Nazis. Pavelić wanted to exterminate the Serbs who lived in Croatia, and he used Hitler as his role model. The Cyrillic alphabet was made illegal, Eastern Orthodox church schools were closed, and Serbs were forced to wear armbands identifying their ethnic background. Thousands of Serbs were driven out of Croatia. Some were forcibly converted to Catholicism, which was the main religion of Croatia. Hundreds of thousands

One Country, Two Masters

In 1941, the Germans and their allies occupied Serbia. To fight the occupation, two resistance groups formed. The Četniks, led by Colonel Draža Mihajlović (seated, second from left), were a predominantly Serbian militia; the Partisans, led by Josip Broz Tito, consisted of Croats, Muslims, and other ethnic groups. The Četniks' and the Partisans' military strategies and ideas of how to run government were quite different. Even so, for a brief period they united their efforts against the Germans and used the slogan, "One Country, Two Masters." It didn't last. The British government initially supported the Četniks, but the Partisans did a better job of fighting the Germans. The British then backed the Partisans and helped them win the civil war. The new Yugoslavia was governed by Tito. Mihajlović was executed by Tito's military and was buried in an unmarked grave.

of Serbs were rounded up in camps and murdered. Jasenovac was one of Pavelić's worst concentration camps.

Though Yugoslavia fell apart, resistance fighters called the Partisans and Četniks were battling the German occupiers—and one another. In 1945, Germany surrendered to the Allied Powers. The Partisans won the civil war against the Četniks and formed a new Yugoslavia, governed by Josip Broz Tito.

The Second Yugoslavia, 1945–1990

In the hands of Tito, Yugoslavia became the Socialist Federal Republic of Yugoslavia. Tito was a Communist, and he used the slogan "in the name of brotherhood and unity" to demand that people set aside their ethnic differences for the good of all.

Josip Broz Tito

Josip Broz was born on May 7, 1892, in Kumrovec, Croatia (then part of Austria-Hungary). His mother was Slovene and his father was a Croatian blacksmith. In the early 1920s, Broz worked as an illegal Communist Party organizer. After he served a prison term (1929–1934), he took the name "Tito" as an alias and went to Moscow to work for the Comintern, an international organization of Communists formed by Vladimir Lenin. Tito ruled Yugoslavia for thirty-five years. He died in 1980.

The Yugoslav government became a one-party Communist regime, and Tito was named president for life. Stores, schools, factories, and offices all displayed his portrait.

In theory, under communism a community, not an individual, owns all the resources and production capabilities in a state or country. Everyone is meant to share the workload, income, production, and resources of the state. The theory founded by Karl Marx and Friedrich Engels assumes that a state-run economy will serve its citizens better than private enterprise will. Tito followed the Soviet model of Communism as developed by Vladimir Lenin, however, Lenin believed in a dictatorship that guided society as it developed into a "communal," or communist, society. As Yugoslavia's dictator, Tito took control of its agricultural land and factories.

In 1946, the Yugoslav government adopted a Constitution similar to that of the Soviet Union, but with an important difference. Unlike other Eastern European Communist countries, Yugoslavia was not a Soviet "satellite"; it did not allow the Soviets to control the economy or its government. In 1948, Josef Stalin, the Communist dictator of the Soviet Union, could no longer tolerate Tito's resistance. He expelled the Yugoslav Communist Party from the Communist Information Bureau (the Cominform).

Tito made some important and positive changes in Yugoslavia. He industrialized the country by building factories and creating jobs. The factories were run by workers' councils, a system of self-management in which workers decided how

The Cominform

the factories should be run. Industrialization improved Yugoslavia's economy. More people could afford luxury items such as washing machines and cars. Health care also improved under Tito. He enacted socialized medicine, making doctors and hospitals available to all citizens. Tito also helped establish the Nonaligned Movement, an alliance of nations that brought him international attention.

Tito's death in 1980 left Yugoslavia without a strong leader. The government adopted a "collective presidency," meaning that each Yugoslav republic had its own representative. Together they decided Yugoslavia's fate. The president of Yugoslavia was selected from this collective group, and the position rotated among the republics. In this way, each republic had a leader as president for a time. By 1990, however, conflicts among the republics erupted, and several declared independence from Yugoslavia.

The Nonaligned Movement

Yugoslavia Splits Again

Slobodan Milošević had risen to power in Serbia in the mid-1980s. He wanted to keep all of Yugoslavia under his control. But in 1991, Slovenia declared independence, followed by Croatia and Macedonia. When Bosnia and Herzegovina did the same, a bitter battle broke out for control of the region. By the end of April 1992, Serbia and Montenegro declared themselves the Federal Republic of Yugoslavia (FRY).

The civil war of the 1990s was tragic for Bosnia and Herzegovina. Many innocent people lost their lives. Most Croatians and Serbs did not want war, but they had little choice.

Milošević had become president of Serbia in 1989. A former Communist bureaucrat, Milošević controlled the republic's media, government appointments, police, and military. He built a Serbian radical nationalist movement. Milošević was responsible, to a great degree, for the violent breakup of Yugoslavia in the early 1990s. His extreme policies in Kosovo plunged Serbia into another bloody battle.

Descent into Madness—War in Kosovo

Milošević's power increased in Kosovo, where about 90 percent of the population is ethnic Albanian. For years, Serbs in the region complained of being harassed, beaten, and forced from their homes by Albanians. Ethnic Albanians had similar complaints, however. They believed that Serbian governmental policies unjustly favored Serbs. Both spoke some truth. The situation in Kosovo grew more tense.

Slobodan Milošević

Slobodan Milošević (right) was born in 1941. He graduated with a degree in law from Belgrade University in 1964. There he met Ivan Stambolić, who became his friend and mentor. In 1986, Stambolić became president of Serbia, and Milošević replaced him as head of the Serbian Communist Party. As tensions grew between the Serbs in Kosovo and the ethnic Albanians who lived there, Milošević fanned the flames of conflict, and criticized Stambolić's regime for its failure to defend Serbian interests in Kosovo. Stambolić was removed from office, and, in 1989, Milošević was elected president of Serbia.

Once the choice of most citizens, Milošević eventually lost popular backing. The civil war in the early 1990s—and the Milošević family's growing stockpile of money and power—distanced the president from the people. In 1996, citizens voiced their outrage over Milošević's policies by electing politicians who opposed him. Milošević declared the local elections invalid. For months, thousands of protesters marched through the streets of Belgrade (below) and other cities.

Milošević's policies in Kosovo sparked international outrage. The United States and the North Atlantic Treaty Organization (NATO) bombed Yugoslavia. They attempted to stop the mass exodus out of Kosovo as people fled Milošević's brutal "cleansing" campaign against ethnic Albanians. The United Nations war crimes tribunal (located in the Hague) issued a warrant for Milošević for "crimes against humanity."

In 2000, Milošević was voted out of office. In 2001, Serb authorities arrested him and handed him over to the United Nations. His trial in the Hague began in 2002.

In April 1987, Milošević gave a speech that ignited the already smoldering flames of ethnic conflict. At the time, public speakers were not allowed to favor one group over another. Public speeches were supposed to foster "brotherhood and unity" and help keep the country together. Milošević broke that rule. He preached the glories of the Serbian nation and proclaimed to the Serbs that "no one will dare beat you again." Serbs saw him as their political savior who could solve the mounting crisis in Kosovo. Unfortunately, he made the situation worse by openly opposing ethnic Albanians.

Milošević took away the autonomous status of Kosovo, pushing it further under Serbia's political thumb. Ethnic Albanians felt the squeeze. Some protested by quitting their jobs; others were fired. Ethnic Albanians created an illegal ("shadow") government and society in Kosovo. They ran their own schools and hospitals, and even collected their own taxes.

In the 1990s, in an attempt to overthrow the Serbian government, a militant group called the Kosovo Liberation Army (KLA) formed an illegal militia. At its strongest, the KLA had about 6,000 recruits. They looted towns and killed Serbian police. The violence exploded into war. Milošević sent the army to rid Kosovo of the KLA by force. Thousands of people died; many others fled or were forced from their homes.

The international community was outraged. The European Community and the United States pressured Milošević and Kosovo Albanian representatives to sign a peace agreement. However, thousands more died or became refugees before peace was established.

The KLA occupied nearly one-third of Kosovo, and Milošević increased his military action. To stop Milošević's army, the North Atlantic Treaty Organization (NATO) bombed Serbia in March 1999. For seventy-eight days, bombs fell upon Kosovo and other Serbian towns, including the capital city of Belgrade. The bombs destroyed bridges, factories, a media center, and other buildings, killing people and critically injuring many. Peace finally came in June 1999, when Milošević agreed to peace terms set by NATO.

To help stabilize the region and create a new government, an international group of armed peacekeepers occupied Kosovo after the peace agreement was signed. Some ethnic Albanian refugees returned, while many Serbs, fearing retaliation, followed the departing Serbian army out of Kosovo.

International aid organizations are still helping Kosovo recover from the war. Kosovo is still a part of Yugoslavia, but an international military force, Kosovo Force (KFOR), remains there to help ensure the peace.

CHAPTER FIVE

Citizens Revolt, a New President Leads

64

A DECADE AND TWO CIVIL WARS LATER Slobodan Milošević was removed from the Yugoslav presidency in 2000—but not without a final conflict. In a general election, citizens voiced their disapproval and voted him out, but Milošević demanded a second election.

His refusal to leave office caused a riot. In Belgrade, thousands took to the streets in protest. Some people threw bricks at government buildings or set fires. They marched in the streets calling for Milošević to step down. Opposition parties called for all citizens to strike. The work stoppage brought the country to a standstill. Milošević finally stepped down. People danced in the streets as Vojislav Kostunica assumed the Yugoslav presidency.

Opposite: **Demonstrators in Belgrade calling for Milošević to step down from office**

Government of the Federal Republic of Yugoslavia

Serbia and Montenegro are the two remaining republics in the Federal Republic of Yugoslavia (FRY). They are reviewing their system of government. Economic reforms are underway, and daily life continues.

Dr. Vojislav Kostunica, President of the FRY

Born in Belgrade in 1944, Dr. Vojislav Kostunica was a deputy in the Parliament of Serbia from 1990 to 1997. He holds a doctorate in law and is the author of many publications in the fields of constitutional law, political theories, and political philosophy. In 1989, he helped create the Democratic Party in Yugoslavia. In 2000 he was elected president of the FRY.

The Federal Assembly building in Belgrade

About 600,000 refugees of various ethnic origins now live in Serbia. The government has given them some support in terms of food and shelter. Most refugees also receive help from their families and neighbors.

Serbia holds most of the power in the FRY. The president of the FRY serves a four-year term. Presidents are elected by direct popular vote, and they can serve up to two consecutive four-year terms.

The Federal Assembly is located in the center of Belgrade. Belgrade is the capital city, political, and administrative center of the FRY and seat of the federal, republic, and city administration. The Federal Assembly consists of two houses—the Chamber of Citizens and the Chamber of Republics. Its members are elected as federal deputies for four-year terms. A prime minister heads the Federal Assembly.

The Federal Assembly is a powerful check on the federal government. It can dismiss the president and members of the federal government if enough deputies cast "no confidence" votes against the federal government.

Under the present Constitution, 30 Federal Assembly deputies come from Montenegro and 108 come from Serbia. The 40 deputies of the Chamber of Republics are elected by the republic assemblies—20 from each republic. Eleven political parties, seven from Serbia and four from Montenegro, take part in the Federal Assembly.

Belgrade: Did You Know This?

In Serbian, Belgrade is *Beograd*, meaning "white city." The city has been known as Belgrade since the ninth century. Its former name was Singidunum. It was first settled in the third or fourth century B.C. by a Celtic tribe called the Scordisci. A large stone fortress surrounds the old part of the city. One of the largest fortifications of its kind in the world, it stands on a bluff above the meeting point of the Danube and the Sava Rivers. The rivers flow north and south of Serbia, making Belgrade a key transportation center. The city has been captured forty times and destroyed thirty-eight times.

A sixteenth-century mosque, a nineteenth-century cathedral, and the Serbian Academy of Sciences are located in Belgrade. The Royal Palace on Dedinje Hill, home to the royal Karadjordjević

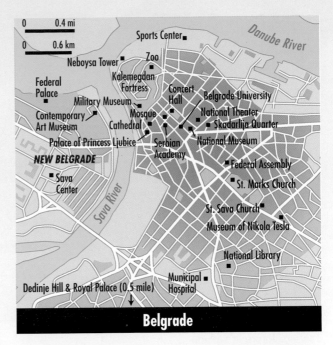

Belgrade

family, overlooks the city. Today, nearly 2 million people live in this modern city, which has many fine museums and shops.

The legislature in session

The Federal Court decides cases that fall under federal law, such as property disputes among republics, as well as cases within the republics and the federal state. This is similar to the duties of the U.S. Supreme Court. The judges of the Federal Court are elected by the Federal Assembly for nine-year terms.

Serbia's Government

Serbia's governmental structure is similar to that of the FRY. It has three branches—executive, legislative, and judicial. The executive branch is made up of the president and the prime minister, deputy prime ministers, and ministers. The president is elected by popular vote for a five-year term and may serve no more than two terms. All ministers are elected by the members of the National Assembly.

The National Assembly is the legislative branch of

NATIONAL GOVERNMENT OF SERBIA

Executive Branch

PRESIDENT

PRIME MINISTER

DEPUTY PRIME MINISTERS (5)

MINISTERS (30)

Legislative Branch

NATIONAL ASSEMBLY (250)

Judicial Branch

CONSTITUTIONAL COURT OF SERBIA

SUPREME COURT OF SERBIA

National Flag

The national flag of Serbia has three horizontal bands colored red, blue, and white. An old folk song describes the colors:

Crvena je krvca bila po Kosovušto se lila;
Plavo nebo ko sloboda ideal je srpskog roda;
Belim mlekom majka mila I mene je zadojila;
Jedan venac—tri su boje, trobojnica srpska to je.

"Red for the blood that was shed in Kosovo,
Blue for heavenly freedom which is Serbia's right,
White is for mother's pure milk that gives life;
One flag with three colors united, that is Serbia."

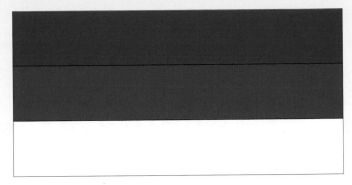

Serbia's government. It has only one house, whose 250 members are elected by the people for four-year terms.

The judicial branch is independent of the executive and legislative branches. It includes the Constitutional Court of Serbia, the Supreme Court of Serbia, and the lower courts.

A Yugoslav army border patrol

Armed Forces

The Yugoslav military is made up of Serbs and Montenegrins. It has army ground forces for internal and border controls, a navy, an air force, and civil defense forces. All Yugoslav males are required to serve twelve months in the armed forces. In addition to a drafted army, paid special forces join the army, the navy, and the air force.

Money,
Money,
Money

Wars are expensive. Soldiers must be paid, weapons and ammunition must be supplied, and tanks and other equipment must be manufactured, delivered, and repaired. Soldiers and civilians may be killed and wounded; property damaged or destroyed. When the conflicts end, buildings, roads, bridges, and other structures must be rebuilt and restored. The rebuilding of war-ravaged Kosovo and Serbia will cost billions of dollars. NATO bombing alone resulted in $60 billion of damage. Who will pay these costs?

Opposite: **It is estimated that rebuilding war-ravaged buildings in Kosovo will cost billions of dollars.**

The wars in Bosnia and Herzegovina and Kosovo were as damaging to Serbia's economy as the Great Depression of the 1930s was to the economy of the United States. They meant long lines at the grocery stores, shortages of all kinds, no gasoline, and the loss of jobs and life savings. The government was slow—or unable—to pay social security checks, and older people who relied on that money had no stable source of income.

People lined up to receive free bread in Belgrade during the economic crisis.

Yugoslavia's Currency

The Yugoslav New Dinar (YUD) is Yugoslavia's currency. There are 100 paras in a dinar. The exchange rate in 2002 was YD60 to $U.S.1. Yugoslavian paper money features the following leaders:

100 dinars–Dositey Obradović, educator instrumental in establishing high schools and promoting literature and poetry

50 dinars–Miloš Obrenović, prince from 1815 to 1839

20 dinars–Djura Jakšić, playwright, poet, and painter

10 dinars–Prince-Bishop Petar Petrović Njegoš, gifted writer, philosopher, and statesman of the nineteenth century; he opened the country's first formal school in 1834

5 dinars–Nikola Tesla, scientist who discovered alternating electrical current (AC)

During the most recent civil wars, inflation rates sky rocketed. Money lost value and prices soared. The price of bread could double in a day, but ration limits restricted people to only one loaf of bread. Essentials like soap and toilet paper became ridiculously expensive. Luxuries such as concerts and trips to the theater were out of reach for many people. A pair of sneakers might cost the equivalent of a month's wages.

Rural dwellers in Serbia provide for themselves by living off the land and raising livestock.

Life in Serbia would have been even more difficult were it not for the country's agricultural bounty. People in rural areas grow much of their own food, and, in season, the earth yields a rich harvest of produce. Fresh water is plentiful, and the countryside is filled with sheep, goats, cattle, and pigs. Nearly every house has a few chickens pecking around its yard.

Economic Sanctions

During wartime, rural citizens in Serbia fared better than those in the cities because they grew and raised their own food. The difficulty was in transporting food to city dwellers. What made it so hard? The United Nations (UN) had imposed economic sanctions that made it illegal for other UN countries to sell gasoline to Serbia. Farmers could still travel by horse and wagon, but that took longer and they couldn't travel as far or carry as much as they could with a motor vehicle. Trucks still ran, but Serbia's gasoline cost three times as much as that of the rest of Europe. Higher gas prices increased the cost of food because of transportation costs. Still, many city people had family in the country, and people took care of one another as best they could.

Economic sanctions are a punishment against a country and an attempt to force its government to comply with certain demands. Serbia was placed under UN sanctions for supporting the Bosnian Serbs during the civil war in the 1990s. The UN imposed a blockade, meaning that Serbia could not trade with other countries. Serbia could not sell its goods, nor could it buy goods from other UN nations, including the former Yugoslav republics.

This was a huge problem for Serbia. For years, industries within the Yugoslav republics were closely linked. For example, the Zastava car plant in central Serbia relied on parts from producers outside its borders. When the federation fell apart, Serbia lost both parts suppliers and car buyers. In 1989, Zastava made 220,000 cars; by 1994, it produced only 7,000.

Economics Exercise

What would massive inflation be like? Say you could buy a compact disc (CD) for $15 one week. The next week, your $15 is worth only $7, but the CD now costs $30. Prices for everything—even food, clothing, medicine, and other essentials were affected in the same way.

While Serbia couldn't trade legally, it also was forbidden to lay off workers. With no way to sell goods, companies struggled to pay their workers. Sometimes they just didn't, but many companies found creative ways to trade goods instead of paying with money. For example, a meat-processing plant needed glue to paste labels on its canned goods. The meat plant traded cans of meat for glue from a glue factory. The meat plant might also partially pay its workers with cans of meat. It wasn't an ideal situation, but at least people didn't starve.

The Black Market

Compact discs for sale on the black market

Black-market trade is the buying and selling of goods without the authority of the government and without paying taxes. For example, people living along the narrowest part of the Danube River in Serbia easily crossed into Romania, where gasoline was less expensive. Riding in small motorboats, they met Romanians in the middle of the river and exchanged empty plastic 1-liter (about 1 quart) bottles for others filled with gasoline. They then sold the gasoline in Serbia for twice what they paid for it. It was a dangerous activity because the highly flammable gasoline was not always stored safely. It was also an illegal activity. Products of all types, from CDs to medical supplies, are still sold on the black market in Serbia.

Employees of this plant hope to have its products exported to neighboring countries.

A Changing Economy

Devastated by economic sanctions and by the criminal activity of government officials, the economy in Serbia needed a massive overhaul. After the UN lifted sanctions in 2000, the new administration began to reform the economy and reduce the unemployment rate, which had reached 30 percent. Foreign investment and trade has resumed. Serbia's economy is slowly improving.

Serbia trades with countries near and far. Export items include machinery and transportation equipment; manufactured goods such as shoes, televisions, cars, and chemicals; as well as food, beverages, livestock, and minerals. A huge hydroelectric dam built in the Djerdap (Iron Gate Gorge) National Park is one of the largest in Europe. It supplies electricity to Yugoslavia and exports power to neighboring countries.

Under the old Yugoslav structure, the government owned most industries. Today, Serbia is moving toward greater privatization, meaning that more people can independently own and manage factories and other businesses.

Agriculture

Serbia has a regular rainfall and a long growing season. About 70 percent of its yield is cereals such as maize, corn, and wheat; 20 percent is industrial herbs; and 10 percent is other crops. Part of the produce is exported, but most of it is processed by the domestic food industry, mainly in Vojvodina. Serbia processes meat, fruit and vegetables, sugar, dairy products, and cotton textiles.

Serbia's main crops include corn, wheat, potatoes, grapes, and animal feed. In addition to modern, large-scale farms,

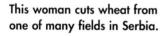
This woman cuts wheat from one of many fields in Serbia.

What Serbia Grows, Makes, and Mines

Agriculture (2000 est.)

Maize and corn	2,937,537 metric tons
Wheat	1,924,385 metric tons
Sugar beets	1,070,033 metric tons
Fruits	816,887 metric tons
Oil seeds	217,608 metric tons

Manufacturing (1993 est.)

Petroleum products	1,983,000 metric tons
Canned meat	10,000 metric tons
Pharmaceuticals	9,500 metric tons
Household appliances	58,000 units
Automobiles	8,000 units

Mining (1993 est.)

Copper	18,189,000 metric tons
Lead and zinc	337,000 metric tons
Lime	318,000 metric tons

Serbia also has many small home gardens. Even city dwellers raise tomatoes, peppers, and fruit trees.

Grapevines and fruit trees have been cultivated in Serbia for more than 2,500 years. Good wines, brandies, and juices come from Fruška Gora and other regions. People also make homemade juices from home-grown fruit.

Kosovo, the southernmost region of Serbia, is the least economically developed. Its land is not fertile, but some fruits, vegetables, tobacco, and a small amount of cereals grow there. The mountainous pastures of Kosovo provide good grazing land for sheep and goats. Some of the region's vineyards are famous for their wines.

HUNGARY

CROATIA

ROMANIA

Wheat O
Beets O
O Corn
Novi Sad
Belgrade
O
C Beets
I O
O
G
Fruits
S Pigs
Danube
Kragujevac
Cu
U
C
BOSNIA
Cr
Sheep
C
M
Timber
C Niš
MONTE-
NEGRO
L Pristina
Peć
Z
C
Z
Z
Cr

ALBANIA   MACEDONIA

Resources

▢ Grain crops	**C**	Coal	**M**	Magnesium	
▢ Mixed farming	**Cu**	Copper	**O**	Oil/Gas	
▢ Vineyards	**Cr**	Chromium	**S**	Silver	
▢ Pastures	**G**	Gold	**U**	Uranium	
▢ Forest	**I**	Iron	**Z**	Zinc	
	L	Lead			

Mining

Rocks may seem worthless, but they can hold hidden treasures. Rocks in Serbia contain valuable deposits of coal, iron, lead, copper, and zinc. In fact, Serbia has the largest copper mine in Europe. In Vojvodina, oil and natural gas deposits lie within the rock. These substances and minerals are mined and processed in factories.

The Kosovo region in particular has a wealth of mineral resources. Miners extract coal, copper, lead, zinc, nickel, chromium, silver, and gold. Steel and aluminum are manufactured as well.

Places to Go, Things to Do

Tourism is still only a small part of Serbia's economy, but it has great potential for growth. The natural beauty of Serbia inspires many outdoor

Mining in Novo Brdo

In the Middle Ages, in the town of Novo Brdo, there was a large silver mine. The town respected and protected its miners. The Code of Novo Brdo required that the miners have safe working conditions and that air shafts be placed in the mines. Mine workers were privileged people at that time. For example, merchants were forbidden to sell food to anyone else if a miner was waiting to buy it.

Kopaonik Resort

Kopaonik Resort is a popular ski center. Even with 200 sunny days a year, it is blanketed with snow from November until May. Skiers from all over Europe enjoy schussing down its slopes. In summer, hikers and horse-back riders follow the trails. Mountain streams sparkle amid tall pines, and edible wild fruits and berries are available for the gathering. You may get lost in these hills, but you won't go hungry.

activities, such as hiking, sailing, rafting, and downhill skiing. Some people visit the northern region to fish; others hunt pheasants, partridges, wild duck, hares, and wild boars.

Serbia's natural hot-spring spas are popular health retreats and tourist centers. Entire towns that cater to tourists have sprung up around these spas. Cultural tours to Serbia's many ancient churches and monasteries are another important part of the tourist industry.

Who Lives in Serbia?

THE MAJORITY OF PEOPLE WHO LIVE IN SERBIA ARE SERBIAN, but other ethnic groups live here, too. The largest groups include Croatians, Hungarians, Romanians, Bosnians, Slovenians, and Albanians. Each has contributed its own cultural flavor to Serbia.

Two areas have especially large concentrations of ethnic groups. The northern Vojvodina Province has a strong Hungarian community; the people in the southern Kosovo Province are nearly all ethnic Albanians. The reason is simple: Both of these provinces border other countries.

Province of Vojvodina

Many Hungarian people live in the northern province of Vojvodina because its capital city, Subotica, borders Hungary. Hungarian influence is everywhere. Hungarian theaters abound, and restaurants serve Hungarian dishes such as goulash, a spicy stew. Many people speak Hungarian, and the language appears on street signs and in newspapers. Even the architecture of Subotica reflects a distinctive Hungarian style.

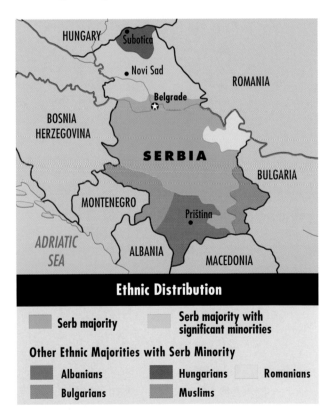

Ethnic Distribution

- Serb majority
- Serb majority with significant minorities

Other Ethnic Majorities with Serb Minority

- Albanians
- Hungarians
- Romanians
- Bulgarians
- Muslims

Regional Pride

An old Serbian saying describes what the people of Šumadija, in central Serbia, are known for: *"Kroz Bosnu ne pevaj, kroz Šumadiju ne igraj!"* Or, "In Bosnia, don't sing; in Šumadija, don't dance!" It means that the people of Bosnia are known to be exceptional singers, while those of Šumadija are skilled dancers.

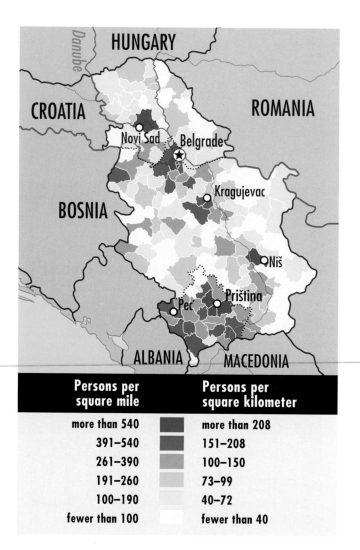

Persons per square mile		Persons per square kilometer
more than 540		more than 208
391–540		151–208
261–390		100–150
191–260		73–99
100–190		40–72
fewer than 100		fewer than 40

Province of Kosovo

Kosovo borders Albania. Centuries ago, the Serbian culture began in the Kosovo region. Today, most of its residents are ethnic Albanians. During the mid-1960s, many Albanians crossed the border and settled in Kosovo. Their traditions and religion are different from those of the Serbs. For example, ethnic Albanians are Muslims, while most Serbs are Orthodox Christians. Serbs usually have families of three or four children, while ethnic Albanians generally have eight or more children. Because ethnic Albanians have larger families, Albanians quickly became the majority population in Kosovo.

The husband and father is the head of the household by ethnic Albanian tradition, and families are tightly knit. Extended families, including cousins, aunts, uncles, and

Albanian men in Kosovo

grandparents, often live in groups of houses surrounded by a thick stone wall or a cement fence.

Though most of the younger generation of Albanians wear Western-style clothing, older women wear traditional clothes that include a head scarf; long, wide pants; and a loose, long-sleeved blouse. Older Albanian men often wear small white caps. The Albanian language is widely spoken throughout Kosovo.

Reading and Writing

The language known as Serbian is spoken throughout Serbia. It is written in two alphabets—Latin, which we use in the West, and Cyrillic. Why two? When Croatia was a part of Yugoslavia, the spoken language was known as Serbo-Croatian, because the

Population of Serbia's Largest Cities (1991 census)*

Belgrade	1,602,226
Novi Sad	179,626
Niš	175,391
Kragujevac	147,305

*Because of the Bosnia and Kosovo wars, this is the last available census figure

Who Lives in Serbia?

Serbs	66%
Albanians	17%
Hungarians	4%
Muslims	3%
Other	10%

This road sign is written in two alphabets, Cyrillic and Latin.

two languages are nearly identical. Croatians were influenced by the Roman Catholic church, so they used the Latin alphabet. Serbs were influenced by the Eastern, or Byzantine, part of the Roman Empire, so they used the Cyrillic alphabet, associated with that part of the world.

The Cyrillic alphabet has thirty letters. Serbian children learn both alphabets in school. Since Serbia split with Croatia in the early 1990s, Serbs tend to use the Cyrillic alphabet more often. Many newspapers, magazines, and street signs are written in Cyrillic. It is Serbia's official alphabet.

Alphabet Roots

The Cyrillic alphabet has a long history and is closely tied to Orthodox Christianity, which was introduced to the Slavs by Greek Byzantine missionaries in the ninth and tenth centuries. At first the missionaries conducted their church services in Greek, which very few Slavs could understand. At that time, the people spoke many Slavic dialects. They could understand one another, but some words and phrases were different from one village to the next. They had no common language or alphabet.

An Alphabet Comparison

The Latin Alphabet	The Cyrillic Alphabet	Pronounced As In
A a	A a	father
B b	Б б	beg
C c	Ц ц	lots
Č č	Ч ч	chime
Ć ć	Ћ ћ	tune
D d	Д д	dog
Dž dž	Џ џ	joy
Đ đ	Ђ ђ	dew
E e	E e	men
F f	Ф ф	fish
G g	Г г	good
H h	Х х	his
I i	И и	she
J j	J j	you
K k	K k	kind
L l	Л л	lake
Lj lj	Љ љ	million
M m	M m	moon
N n	Н н	not
Nj nj	Њ њ	onion
O o	O o	door
P p	П п	pen
R r	Р р	run
S s	C c	son
Š š	Ш ш	she
T t	T т	tag
U u	У у	rule
V v	В в	very
Z z	З з	zoo
Ž ž	Ж ж	leisure

A statue of Cyril and Methodius, creators of the Cyrillic alphabet

Byzantine missionaries Cyril and Methodius created the basis for what is now known as the Cyrillic alphabet. Thus began the literary language of the church, called Old Church Slavonic. The idea of using one language to communicate church teachings also worked in Western Europe, where Latin was used.

English Is Everywhere

Other languages are spoken in Serbia, including English. Though most Serbs are not fluent in English, some English words have slipped into the Serbian language. Words like *hamburger*, *computer*, and *drugstore* are used in everyday conversation. American culture has also influenced

One Sound for One Letter

"Write the way you speak. Read as it is written." That was Vuk Karadzić's philosophy for spelling. In the nineteenth century, Karadzić reformed the Serbian language and wrote the first Serbian dictionary, using a phonetic spelling system. This greatly simplified the language and made it easier to learn. Every letter has just one sound. Each word is spelled as it sounds, with the emphasis usually on the first syllable.

English vowels can be long or short, and the language has silent letters, such as "gh" in the word "thigh." If English were a phonetic language, "thigh" would simply be spelled "thi."

A few English phrases spelled phonetically from the Serbian point of view appear below. Sound them out to see what they mean. (Hint: "j" is pronounced like "y" and "i" is pronounced "ee.")

Tu bojs end thri gerls
Bi gud to jur self.
Aj dont no.

lifestyles in Serbia, especially in the cities. You'll see people in American-style dress and see fast-food restaurants, and you'll hear plenty of American music. Of course, the influences of other European nations on Serbia are also very strong. You can buy Italian shoes, German electronics, and delicious Swiss chocolates in Serbia.

Weights and Measures

Like most of the world, Serbia uses the metric system. Weight is measured in kilograms, distances in kilometers, and temperatures in Celsius. The metric system was introduced in France in 1799. Most countries adopted it as the common system of weights and measures.

All countries use the metric system as an international standard for science. For example, computer memory capacity is expressed as gigabytes. "Giga" comes from the metric system and means 1 billion. The United States has tried many times to convert to the metric system, but it hasn't succeeded yet.

Serbia has many social and cultural traditions. For example, when you enter a Serbian home for the first time, it is customary to bring a small gift, such as flowers, a bottle of wine, or some chocolates for the children. You would likely take off your shoes when you enter and leave them in the doorway. Hosts provide slippers for you to wear, since most people don't go barefoot in their homes.

Shoes are left in the doorway of this home.

In Serbia, it is also customary to serve food and drink to guests. You might be served a sweet called *slatko*, which is a delicious fruit preserve, often made of strawberries. In both city and country homes, slatko is served on a small silver tray lined with a lace doily. Serbs are gracious hosts and make visitors feel special and welcome.

Serbs celebrate their cultural heritage with festivals. They wear traditional costumes and enjoy folk music, traditional dances, and special foods.

Greetings!

If you've ever had a problem remembering someone's name, you might want to try the Serbian style of greeting. When you are introduced to someone in Serbia, you shake hands, and both you and the other person say your own first and last names. Saying a person's name aloud helps you remember it.

Traditions, Faith, and Folklore

THE PEOPLE OF SERBIA FOLLOW THREE RELIGIONS: Eastern Orthodoxy, Roman Catholicism, and Islam. Orthodoxy and Catholicism follow the teachings of Jesus Christ. Islam is based on the teachings of the prophet Muhammad.

At one time, there was only one Christian church. In 1054, the church powers in Rome and Constantinople battled for political control and split in two. This "Great Schism" separated these two Christian churches into the Roman Catholic and Byzantine (Eastern Orthodox) Church.

Opposite: **Saint Archangel Michael Cathedral Church, Belgrade**

Orthodoxy

While there are differences between Orthodoxy and Catholicism, the root of their beliefs is the same. One difference, however, is that Orthodox priests may marry, but Roman Catholic priests may not.

Most people in Serbia are Orthodox Christians. The Orthodox religion is tied to the beginnings of the Serbian state. The Serbian Orthodox Church was established in 1219, about the time when Serbia was recognized as an independent state. The Nemanja family followed Orthodox teachings and built several elaborate monasteries.

Stefan Nemanja, the first king of Serbia, was crowned in 1217. His brother later achieved sainthood and carried the name Saint Sava. Though he was born to a very wealthy and powerful family, Sava chose to dedicate his life to the

Religions of Yugoslavia*	
Eastern Orthodox	65%
Islamic	19%
Roman Catholic	4%
Protestant	1%
Other	11%

*Statistics include Serbia and Montenegro.

A Shining Masterpiece in Topola

On top of Oplenac Hill in Topola sits the glorious Church of Saint George and the mausoleum of the Karadjordjević Dynasty. It was built in the early 1900s, but modeled after old medieval Serbian monasteries.

The interior is covered in mosaics, gold, and carved marble. The mosaics are made of 40 million glass pieces in 15,000 hues, and the images portray historic and religious events.

heavenly kingdom. He was a religious man and very well educated. He taught the Serbian people religious values and also helped educate them. Over time, people followed his teachings, and the church became extremely important to the Serbian people. Saint Sava's words gave Serbs great comfort in difficult times. When the Turks conquered Serbia, they allowed the Serbian Orthodox Church to continue. The religion helped to unite the Serbs and keep their culture alive during the long years of Ottoman rule.

Saint Sava

Though more than 700 years have passed since the death of Saint Sava, his teachings still influence Serbian people. Many churches have been dedicated to Saint Sava in Serbia and throughout the world, especially in the United States and Canada. Saint Sava is the patron saint of Serbia. When the magnificent Saint Sava Church in Belgrade is completed, it will be the largest of its kind. The Orthodox priests shown here are standing beneath a portrait of Saint Sava.

Muslim men pray at a mosque in Priština

The Five Pillars of Islam

Islam was introduced to the inhabitants of the Balkan region centuries ago by Ottoman Turks. The Islamic holy book is known as the Koran. People who follow the teachings of Islam are called Muslims.

Five duties are required of all Muslims. The first is to publicly declare their creed, which says that Allah is the one God and Muhammad is his prophet. The second duty is to say five daily prayers: before sunrise, in early afternoon, in late afternoon, immediately after sunset, and before retiring. The third duty is to give money to the poor, and the fourth is to fast during the month of Ramadan. The fifth duty is to make a pilgrimage to Mecca at least once, if not prevented by ill health or poverty.

The religion is still practiced in Serbia today. Most Muslims live in the Kosovo Province.

Christmas Eve at Home

After church on Christmas Eve, everyone brings home some oak branches and bunches of straw. The children gather behind their father and follow him to the door of their home. The father makes a clucking sound, while the children pretend to be little chicks and cry "peeyoo, peeyoo, peeyoo!" The father knocks on the door three times, and the mother answers and welcomes them inside. The branches and straw symbolize the manger where Christ was born.

Serbs are a passionate people, and that quality is evident in their celebrations. Rich cultural traditions play a part in holidays, weddings, and special relationships. Serbs and some other Orthodox Christians throughout the world celebrate Christmas on January 7 instead of December 25. The date is different because the Orthodox follow a different, older calendar for their holy days.

The Serbian word for Christmas is *Božić*. It comes from the word *Bog*, or God, and means "Infant God." On Christmas morning in Serbia, you don't just wake up and tear into gifts. Instead, you wait for someone to bring Christmas into your house. This "someone" is a specially selected young child or neighbor who knocks on the door to "bring in the spirit of Christ." The youngster pokes a stick into the fireplace, and the number of sparks that fly up indicates how much luck the family will have in the year ahead. The young person is given gifts in thanks for bringing the spirit of Christ into the home.

A Serbian Orthodox Christmas Eve is a special event. The evening is called *Badnje Vece* (BUD-neyea vech-eh). *Badnjak* means "yule log." People carry branches of an oak tree to the church courtyard and make a bonfire. Neighbors, friends, and families gather around the fire as the priest blesses it, and the church choir sings Christmas hymns. The burning of the yule log symbolizes Christ, who is said to give light in darkness and warmth against cold. After the ceremony, people gather in the church hall to chat and eat Lenten foods (no meat or dairy products). Adults also enjoy a special drink called a "hot toddy," which consists of heated brandy sweetened with honey.

The main foods of the Christmas feast are roast pork and a special bread called *česnica* (CHES-nee-tsa). This delicious round bread is decorated with special symbols, and baked with a coin inside. When the bread is broken apart, the person who gets the piece with the coin is said to have good luck for the coming year.

Česnica bread

A Saint to Watch Over the Family

Slava means "giving thanks." In Serbian tradition, every family has a patron saint who protects them. The family honors their special saint on a day called *Krsna Slava*, "Patron Saint Day." These celebrations occur throughout the year, and the tradition is passed down from father to son. It is a day of feasting and giving thanks for all the good things in life. Family and friends are all invited to celebrate.

Religious rituals for Slava include the lighting of a special candle, which symbolizes the positive light of the patron saint shining through the day. A Slava *kolać* (ko-lach), a round bread, and a *žito* (zhee-toe), boiled, sweetened wheat, are also prepared. Each guest takes a small spoonful of wheat in memory of those who have passed away.

On Slava, a priest comes into the house and blesses all the rooms with holy water and incense to keep out evil spirits. The family and priest gather in a circle and turn the Slava

kolać around while they sing a special song. The priest blesses the bread with wine, and the father or the oldest son breaks the bread in half. Each member of the family kisses the bread while the priest says, "God is in our midst." Each family member responds, "He is and always will be."

For the Souls of the Dearly Departed

Funerals in Serbia are elaborate affairs, and many people are invited to attend the burial. At the burial site, tables are set for a lavish meal of salads and roasted meats to honor the person who died. A similar large gathering is held after one year, when the gravestone is placed. In addition to inscriptions, photos are placed on gravestones.

Kumovi—An Extension of Family

Many centuries ago, when Christians began to baptize children, the custom of a sponsor was introduced. That sponsor was called the godfather. In Serbian he is called *kum* (koom), and the godmother is *kuma*. *Kumovi* (koo-moh-vee), or godparents, are responsible for the baby should anything happen to the parents. Kumovi also have the privilege of naming the child.

Kumovi become valued members of the family. They are not blood relatives, but they are just as important. Kumovi are treated as well-respected "spiritual" family members. This Serbian expression reveals how important the kum is: "God in heaven and the kum on Earth."

Serbs have kumovi for weddings too. In Vojvodina, kumovi have an honored wedding seat. An old tradition requires

that no one eat a bite until after the kum or kuma of the wedding has begun to eat. When the kumovi leave the reception, they are not allowed to walk on the ground. They walk on chairs placed from the reception hall to a waiting car, and musicians serenade them all the way out.

In the villages, wedding celebrations can last several days. Guests generally stay with family and close friends during this time. After the couple returns from their honeymoon, the bride stands at the doorway of her new house. She lifts a baby boy three times and asks that her marriage be blessed with children.

Folktales

Folktales teach moral values and often feature animals or people with special powers. Some stories are meant to teach children to behave by telling them that a "boogie man" will get them if they don't. The Serbian version of the boogie man is called "Baba Roga." She is an ugly old witch who is said to take bad children away from their families if they don't listen to their mother and father.

A watercolor of Baba Roga by Dragan Kecman

Another popular folktale features a dog and a piece of meat: One day a dog was carrying a piece of delicious meat in his mouth. As he was crossing a mountain stream, he looked down and saw his own reflection. He thought the reflection was another dog with an even larger piece of meat. When he tried to grab it, he dropped his own meat and the stream carried it away. The dog tried to blame the river for stealing his food, but the river told him that if he weren't so greedy, he wouldn't have lost his meat in the first place.

Pictures, Words, and Music

THE ART OF SERBIA HAS NOT ONLY BEEN INFLUENCED BY others (especially the Byzantines in the early centuries), but it has also contributed to various European art movements. Among the more significant kinds of art is sacred, or religious, art. Frescoes and mosaics adorn the walls, floors, and ceilings of monasteries and churches throughout Serbia.

The word *fresco* means "fresh" in Italian. It is a method of painting with watercolors on wet plaster. Mosaics are made of small pieces of colored glass, stone, ceramic, or other materials. In some of Serbia's churches, gold leaf was used in mosaic art.

A mosaic of Jesus Christ

Opposite: **Religious art is presented in frescoes throughout Serbia's monasteries and churches.**

A Gathering Place for Artists

Skadarlija (SKA-dar-lee-ya) was a gathering place in Belgrade for famous writers and artists at the end of the nineteenth century. A brewery at the end of Skadarska Street, which gave the neighborhood its name, inspired many taverns, restaurants, and shops to open there.

Today people of all ages meet in Skadarlija to sip coffee, browse art galleries, eat good food, and enjoy plays and cabarets.

Painting Today

Serbia's strong artistic heritage is very much alive today. You can see both modern and historic elements in contemporary paintings, including elements of the ancient Lepenski Vir

Dragan Kecman

Dragan "Joyce" Kecman is among the up-and-coming artists in Serbia. He was born in the small town of Kučevo, where he now has a studio and an exhibition gallery. His images appear to be gently floating in space, giving his paintings a part-reality, part-dream quality. His work is collected by art lovers around the world.

rocks, Byzantine styles, religious ideas, and surrealism (fantasy). Well-known Serbian artists who have exhibited their work around the world include the late Milan Konjović, who favored bright colors and nature motifs, and Milić Stanković, whose works include oil paintings of Serbian life and fine illustrations. Olja Ivanićki's paintings include figurative and surrealistic images.

Folk Arts and Crafts

Art can be both decorative and practical. In Serbia, the applied arts include textiles, pottery, etched crystal, intricate lacework, and carved and inlaid wood. The design, or architecture, of buildings and churches can also be considered practical art.

Serbia's textiles are made from its abundant supply of wool, flax, and hemp. The handmade carpets are colorful and very durable. They are often composed with geometric patterns such as zig-zags, squares, and steps. These rugs are still available today, mostly in the markets of smaller towns and villages.

Egg decoration has long been popular with the Slavic people. In old

Folk textiles of Serbia

Folk Textiles.

Decorated eggs of Serbia

Serbia, natural dyes were used. Boiled onion peelings turned the eggs a lovely amber or pale yellow, depending on the type of onion skin.

Egg Tapping

Serbian Easter includes a special ritual with decorated Easter eggs. Children and adults tap their eggs against each other to see which egg is strongest. One person holds an egg in his fist with only the tip showing while another person taps it with the tip of her own egg. The winner is the person whose egg does not crack. As you might imagine, a lot of eggs get smashed. Children and adults look forward to this fun ritual every year.

Literature

It is said that painting is like visual poetry, and that poetry paints pictures. Serbia has a long literary history. From the thirteenth-century epic poetry of Kosovo to modern novels, Serbs love to tell a good story. In the 1800s, two great poets were recognized beyond the borders of Serbia—Jovan Jovanović Zmaj and Djura Jakšić.

Isidora Sekulić (1877–1958) was the first woman to become a member of the Serbian Academy of Arts and Sciences. By the time she was fourteen, she was fluent in five languages—German, French, Russian, Italian, and Serbian. She was known for her original stories and her ability to translate difficult writings. One day while she was strolling through a park in Belgrade, an officer of King Aleksandar invited her to visit the monarch. She thought it over for a moment, then said, "Please tell the king not to be offended, but I have no time for him at the moment." She then continued her walk through the park, perhaps thinking over a story line for her next piece of writing.

A Song of Times Past

A *gusle* (goos-la) is a traditional one-stringed instrument.

Grandfather and Grandson

The grandfather took his grandson
Put him on his knee,
And with gusle he did sing
Of all that used to be.

He sang to him of Serbian glory
Serbian knights of old
He sang to him of battles fierce
And suffering untold.

And grandfather's eye did glisten
As he shed a tear
And then his little grandson bade
To kiss the gusle dear.

The child did kiss the ancient gusle
Then he asked in bliss
"Tell me, Grand-dad, why did I
The gusle yonder kiss?"

"You know not, my little Serb
But we, your elders do.
When you grow up and think it through
It will all just come to you."

—Jovan Jovanović Zmaj

(Courtesy of *Little Falcons Magazine*, edited by Father Thomas Kazich, Grayslake, Ill.)

The world has recognized many excellent Serbian writers. Mihajlo Pupin, a Serbian scientist who immigrated to the United States in 1874, was also a distinguished writer. He won a Pulitzer Prize for his autobiography, *From Immigrant to Inventor*. In his book he talks about what made him curious. "Herding oxen with other village boys, I watched stars at night and thought their light was a language of God. . . . I didn't know how that language reached me and hoped someday that I might find out." He found answers to his questions. Pupin became a famous professor of physics at Columbia University in New York City. Today, you can see a building on the campus that is dedicated to him.

In 1961, Ivo Andrić, a Bosnian Serb, became the first Yugoslav to receive a Nobel Prize. He is the author of *Bridge over the River Drina*. Other popular authors today include Milorad Pavic and Vladimir Arsenijević, whose books have been translated into many languages.

Nobel Prize–winner Ivo Andrić (second from left)

Stories on Screen

Films made by Serbian directors have been exported to other countries. They are often produced on very small budgets, especially compared with those of multimillion-dollar Hollywood films. But the emotional power of the stories told in Serbian films can make them as moving as the most costly blockbusters.

When we talk about the history of filmmaking in Serbia, we need to do so from the point of view of Yugoslavia. Remember, it once had six republics within it, though only two remain today. The funds, talent, and production centers for filmmaking developed across Yugoslavia as a whole.

The first Serbian film recordings began in 1905. The filmmaker Milton Manaki started by simply shooting some scenes of ordinary life in his small town. His first full-length film, completed in 1910, told the story of the Serbian Karadjordjević Dynasty. It was a coproduction between Belgrade and Paris, France.

The films produced during World Wars I and II were mostly educational, tourist, and war-documentary films. The film industry began to expand in 1945, when the Yugoslav government began to pay for productions. By the 1960s, Yugoslavia's economy had improved, and the number of film products increased along with it.

The world really began to take notice of Yugoslav filmmaking in the 1980s. The most influential director was Emir Kusturica, who was born in Sarajevo in 1955. His films were about human relationships and struggles with the government.

A Filmmaker's View

"I believe everyone has a special gift that has to be given away to the world. The more of it you give, the more you discover yourself. The more of yourself that you discover, the more you want to give away. That is, I believe, the great purpose of life."

–Zoran Maširević, television and film director

Kusturica's American Period

In the early 1990s, the famous director Emir Kusturica spent several years in the United States teaching filmmaking at Columbia University in New York. During that time he shot *Arizona Dreaming* (1993), a movie featuring Johnny Depp, Faye Dunaway, and Jerry Lewis.

His second film, *When Father Was Away on Business* (1985), won first place at the Cannes Film Festival. He was the first director to show openly why people feared Communism and how innocent citizens were imprisoned for no reason. He greatly influenced many directors. He often worked with musical composer Goran Bregović. That partnership proved successful for both of them. A number of Kusturica's films are available in the United States with English subtitles.

Though the civil war in the 1990s reduced the number of films being produced in Serbia, creativity did not diminish. Comedies, tragedies, and romances still premiered on subjects such as love, greed, adventure, and disaster. Especially popular were films about the war, showing how ordinary people were affected by the tragedy.

Perhaps more than any other subject, Serbian filmmakers are masters at revealing the depth and drama of human relationships. Because these films are so powerful, many viewers walk away with a new outlook on the world. One such powerful film is *Pretty Villages, Pretty Flames* (1996), directed by Srdjan

Dragojević. Based on a true story, the film focuses on two young men who were best friends all their lives. One of them is a Serb and the other is a Muslim. When civil war hits their town—a war among Serbs, Croats, and Muslims—the young men are caught in the middle of the conflict and must choose between their friendship and the politics of war. The film was praised by critics worldwide and attracted the attention of Hollywood agents.

Zoran Maširević is another Serbian television and film director whose work reveals how war affects ordinary people. His film *The Border* (1990) is set on the border between Yugoslavia and Hungary and takes place between 1945 and 1948, when the two countries were at odds. World War II has ended, but people are still angry. A young Yugoslav boy falls in love with a Hungarian girl. At first, their families refuse to let the young couple be together. But they find a way to see each other. Eventually they marry, and their union draws the families together as well. *The Border* won numerous awards and has played around the world. Maširević now lives and works in Los Angeles, California.

Film director Srdjan Dragojević

Actors and Screenwriters

Well-known American actors of Serbian descent include John Malkovich (above left), Karl Malden, and Lolita Davidovich (above right). Steven Tesich is an Academy Award–winning screenwriter.

American actors have also appeared in Yugoslav films. Brad Pitt's first starring role in a feature film was in the 1988 Yugoslav production *The Dark Side of the Sun*.

Music

Music has been called the universal language. Like other arts in Serbia, its history began a long time ago. In the thirteenth century, musicians who played the *gusle*, called *guslari* (GOOS-la-ree), were like newscasters. They traveled from village to village singing ballads about current events and history.

Tamburitza orchestras play another kind of folk music on special string instruments similar to mandolins and banjos. The musicians, called *tamburashi* (tom-BOO-rah-she), are highly skilled and play with energy and enthusiasm. Often, three or four musicians get together at a social event to play, while people dance and sing along. The festivities may last late into the evening.

A gusle player

Muscians entertain diners in a Serbian restaurant

Tipping Tamburashi

If someone requests a song in Serbia, he or she tips the musicians in an amusing way. The person places a bill on the neck of the instrument or sticks the money onto the perspiring forehead of the musician.

Founded in May 1989, B92 began as a student-run radio station. Today, it is a multimedia force at the forefront of arts and communications. Milošević censored the media during his rule, but thanks to the Internet, B92 bypassed the censorship and brought many young people together.

B92 fosters arts and culture through radio, Internet, music, film, and publishing projects. You can listen to its broadcasts at www.b92.net.

Today in Serbia, all kinds of music can be heard on the radio. What's interesting is the mix—everything from traditional folk music to rock to classical music—often played on the same station. Serbia imports a great deal of popular music from the United States and Britain, but it has its own pop stars, too. The popular radio station B92 broadcasts from Belgrade and worldwide on the Internet.

Dance

Serbia celebrates dance with formal ballet performances at the National Theater in Belgrade and with folklore groups that

What Do Teenagers Listen To?

Young Serbs listen to everything from pop to rap, including the music of Michael Jackson, Madonna, Celine Dion, and C-Block. Bands like *Bjelo Dugme* (White Button) and *Ribja Corba* (Fish Stew) are among the well-known Yugoslav rock musicians. They incorporate American rock with ethnic Serbian sounds. Their music is available on audiocassettes and compact discs.

travel around the country. *Kolos* are traditional Serbian circle dances. They are performed by professional troupes and ordinary citizens. Dancers hold hands and form a half-circle. One person leads the string of dancers around the floor. Everyone dances together—grandmothers, teen-

Yugoslav folk dancers

age boys, girls, aunts, and neighbors.

Kolos are most often performed at weddings and other special gatherings. Some are slow; others are fast and require fancy footwork as well as good aerobic conditioning. Dancing a few of the faster kolos is as good as jogging a mile or more.

Images of people dancing kolos appear in old frescoes. The Ottoman Turks who once occupied Serbia were very strict. During their rule, people were not allowed to gather to talk, but they could socialize on special occasions. The kolo dances were a way for people to communicate. They would send messages to one another through the lyrics in the music.

In Serbian towns and cities today, young people dance at discos on Saturday nights. A variety of popular music is played, most of it rock-based, but Serbian discos differ from those in the United States. In Serbia, young people of all ages are allowed to enter discos. When a well-known song is played, many people sing along. And girls don't wait for boys to ask them to dance—it is totally acceptable for girls to dance together.

At Home, School, and Play

114

I N A PATERNALISTIC SOCIETY, A WOMAN TAKES HER HUSBAND'S last name in marriage, and the husband is considered the head of the household. It is his responsibility to work and provide food and shelter for his family. Serbian society is paternalistic, but today, many women work outside the home, too. An old Serbian saying declares that the husband is the head of the house and the woman is the foundation. In other words, it takes both husband and wife to make a successful family. Each contributes to the welfare of their home and children.

Families in Serbia tend to be very close-knit. It is not unusual to find parents, their adult children, and even grand-children living together in the same home. Even when they do not share a home, family members often stay close to where they were born. Cousins, aunts, uncles, and grandparents may all live in the same town, perhaps even next door.

In the Serbian language, there is no direct translation for the word *cousin*. Cousins are called sisters or brothers. Although that may cause some confusion about family rela-tionships, it also creates a special closeness.

Games

Many of the games children play in Serbia are like those chil-dren play in the United States and Canada. Hide-and-seek, hopscotch, and jump rope are popular. Video games are also popular, especially in the cities. Young Serbs spend hours on

A group of friends gathers for an informal soccer game

the Internet, too. They play basketball and *fudbal* (food-bawl), which is what they call soccer. Soccer is very popular throughout Serbia. Most communities have athletic leagues for children aged five to fifteen. The basketball court and the soccer field are popular places after school. Some children attend summer basketball camps. Serbian basketball stars such as Sacramento Kings player Vlade Divac hold workshops especially for children.

Serbian Basketball Stars

A number of Serbian athletes play basketball on American teams. Vlade Divac (bottom left), born in Serbia, plays center for the Sacramento Kings and is ranked fifth in the NBA triple doubles. Predrag Stojankovic, born in 1977 in Belgrade, also plays for the Sacramento Kings. He was the Kings' first-round draft choice when he was just nineteen years old. In the 1970s and 1980s, basketball superstar Pete Maravich (bottom right), born in the United States to Serbian parents, played for the Atlanta Hawks and the Boston Celtics. He was called "Pistol Pete" for his bullet speed. Maravich was inducted into the NBA Hall of Fame in 1987.

Professional soccer, hockey, and basketball are among the most popular spectator sports in Serbia. The Yugoslav Olympic basketball team came very close to beating the U.S. team in the 1996 Olympics and won the silver medal. The Serbs are also well known for their rifle-shooting skills. Serbian women have earned Olympic gold medals in that sport—Aleksandra Ivošev in 1996 and Jasna Sekarić in 1992. Handball, water polo, and volleyball are other sports at which Serbian athletes excel.

Aleksandra Ivošev

A Belgrade café

Meeting Friends

Whether visiting one another for afternoon coffee or meeting later in the evening, Serbs love to socialize. After dinner on warm summer evenings, every town has a *korzo* (KOHR-zo). The main street is closed to traffic, and people slowly stroll the street, greeting neighbors and friends. Both children and adults come out for korzo.

The main street of most towns is lined with cafés, or *kafanas* (ka-FUN-ahs). Serbs love their cafés. Now that the government allows people to own private businesses, you see cafés on almost every corner. People stop for a Turkish coffee or perhaps a refreshing fruit drink called a *sok* (sawk).

A Kiss Hello

Friends and family members kiss each other as a greeting. Men kiss men, and women kiss women. They give three kisses in all—first one cheek, then the other, then the first cheek again.

Primary school students

Education

Schools are free in Serbia, but schoolwork is very demanding. Serbian students who have come to the United States to study have often remarked how much easier it is to earn high marks. In Serbia, school is mandatory up to age sixteen.

After the first eight years of school, most children attend secondary school (*sredjna skola*), where they select a skilled vocation or a field for advanced education. They attend secondary school for three or four years, depending on the chosen vocation. Students can study anything from electronics to medicine. After secondary school, they have enough knowledge and skills to get a job. They may also choose to go to a university and continue their studies.

About one-third of Serbian pupils attend *gimnazija*, which provides them with a broad academic education. Requirements in gimnazija include Latin, philosophy, art, and biology classes. After these studies, students go to university. The main difference between srednja skola and gimnazija is that srednja skola trains students to enter the work force, while gimnazija prepares them for intensive university study. Studies at a university last four to six years, depending on the field of study.

Serbian National Holidays

New Year	January 1
Day of Statehood	February 15
International Labor Day	May 1
Day of Uprising	July 7
Republic Day	November 29

A Mathematical Genius Helps Einstein

Born in Serbia, Mileva Marić was one of the first women admitted to the prestigious Swiss Federal Polytechnic School in 1896. She excelled in math and science. At the institute she met her husband, Albert Einstein. The two were married in 1903 and had two sons. During their marriage, Mileva, a mathematical genius, contributed to Einstein's famous theories.

At Home

Most Serbian homes are smaller than those in the United States and Canada. Children often share a bedroom. Kitchens are for food preparation only, and families eat meals in a dining room.

Today, most city dwellings have central heat, but in smaller towns, people still use coal or wood to heat their homes. Though stoves heat homes fairly well, electric heaters are quickly replacing them because they are much more

Outside a small town Serbian home

convenient. There's no wood to chop and no messy black coal to store and handle.

Electricity is commonly available. In fact, Serbia built one of Europe's largest hydroelectric stations on the Danube River at the Iron Gate Gorge. People in Serbia use electricity to power everything from blow-dryers to telephone answering machines to computers. A famous Serbian engineer and inventor by the name of Nikola Tesla contributed greatly to the evolution of the electrical current we all use today.

Nikola Tesla (1856–1943)

Nikola Tesla emigrated to the United States after completing his science studies in Europe. He worked for a short time with Thomas Edison, who called Tesla "a poet of science." The two eventually became rivals. Tesla's idea of connecting alternating current (AC) to a motor led to the development of power stations in the United States and around the world. Tesla received 112 U.S. patents for his discoveries and inventions. A statue honoring him was erected at Goat Island power station, Niagara Falls.

The tasty food served throughout Serbia focuses on the basic food groups: vegetables and fruits, meats, dairy, and breads. Though rice and pasta are available, Serbs do not eat them in great abundance. Breakfast often includes eggs, meat, and bread, and sometimes yogurt and cheese. *Kajmak* (KAY-mak) is a Serbian specialty. It tastes like a blend of butter and cream cheese. People use kajmak in baked goods and as a spread for bread.

Serbs eat the main meal of the day in the afternoon, at about 3:00 P.M., after schools and businesses let out. The workday generally runs from 8:00 A.M. to 2:00 P.M. with no lunch break; people often work a half day on Saturdays. What do people eat at their main meal? Usually quite a bit! Roasted meats or stews, cheeses, and freshly baked bread are a typical afternoon meal. Of course, after such a hearty meal many people take a brief nap. Dinner is usually a lighter meal, eaten about eight o'clock in the evening.

Eating in Serbia in the summertime is a delicious experience. Locally grown fruits and vegetables are abundant. Many people tend gardens and grow flowers and vegetables such as tomatoes, green onions, and peppers. Peppers are used in many dishes—they are stuffed with special meats and baked, pickled in a jar, or simply sliced fresh and added to tomatoes and onions.

Serbia has a number of national specialties. *Proja* is a corn bread with kajmak cheese and ham, and *gibanica* is crispy, paper-thin dough layered with cheese and egg. Serbia's spiced

Peppers for sale at a market

Čevapčiči

Čevapčiči (chee-VAHP-chee-chee) are small sausages made of pork, lamb, beef, and spices. When they are grilled outdoors, you can smell the scent for blocks. Čevapčiči are eaten with fresh bread and diced white onions.

A waiter serves a Serbian favorite, palačinke

sausages are delicious, and so are *sarma*—meat-stuffed cabbage leaves—and *djuveć*, a tomato-based vegetable stew. Desserts include dry *pita* (strudel) with walnuts, apples, or sour cherries, and *palačinke* (crepes).

Beating the Summer Heat

Air-conditioning is not common in Serbia. To escape the summer heat, people stay in the shade when possible. They grow

grapevines, which produce lots of green leaves, on wooden frames to make their own shade. Families place picnic tables under this cool green canopy. To avoid heating the indoors, people barbecue outside.

To avoid the heat, many Serbs barbecue under a shady tree.

How to Make a Palačinka

A *palačinka* (pah-lah-CHEEN-ka) is a crepe, basically a thin pancake, and very easy to make. This recipe makes 4 or 5 palačinke (*palačinke* is the plural).

   1 egg
   1 cup milk
   1 cup flour
   cooking oil
   jam
   powdered sugar
   frying pan a bit smaller than a dinner plate

Add 1 egg to 1 cup of milk and beat well. Then add 1 cup of flour and blend. The mixture should be thinner than pancake batter. Heat a tablespoon of oil in a frying pan until it begins to crackle. Pour about 1/4 cup of the mixture into the pan and spread it around to make a thin layer on the bottom of the pan. When the color changes to a deeper yellow and the mixture looks firm, flip it with a spatula. It will fry quickly on the second side. Flip the palačinka onto a plate. Fry the rest of the batter the same way, adding oil if needed. Once the palačinke have cooled, spread them with a tablespoon each of your favorite jam. Fold them in half lengthwise, then fold across. Sprinkle with a little powdered sugar and enjoy!

Timeline

Serbian History		World History	
Stone Age community settles at Lepenski Vir.	7000 B.C.		
		2500 B.C.	Egyptians build the Pyramids and the Sphinx in Giza.
		563 B.C.	The Buddha is born in India.
		A.D. 313	The Roman emperor Constantine recognizes Christianity.
		610	The Prophet Muhammad begins preaching a new religion called Islam.
		1054	The Eastern (Orthodox) and Western (Roman) Churches break apart.
		1066	William the Conqueror defeats the English in the Battle of Hastings.
		1095	Pope Urban II proclaims the First Crusade.
Nemanja Dynasty begins.	A.D. 1168		
Stefan Nemanja is crowned as Serbia's first king.	1217	1215	King John seals the Magna Carta.
Serbian Orthodox Church established.	1219		
		1300s	The Renaissance begins in Italy.
Battle of Kosovo.	1389	1347	The Black Death sweeps through Europe.
Ottoman Empire rules Serbia.	1389–1815		
		1453	Ottoman Turks capture Constantinople, conquering the Byzantine Empire.
		1492	Columbus arrives in North America.
		1500s	The Reformation leads to the birth of Protestantism.
		1776	The Declaration of Independence is signed.
Serbian leader Miloš Obrenović leads revolt.	1815	1789	The French Revolution begins.
		1865	The American Civil War ends.

Serbian History		World History	
Serbia regains independence following the Ottoman Empire's defeat by Russia and Serbia.	1878		
During Balkan Wars, Serbia and other Balkan countries gain control of most Ottoman Empire possessions in Europe.	1912		
Austria declares war on Serbia, starting World War I.	1914	1914	World War I breaks out.
		1917	The Bolshevik Revolution brings communism to Russia.
Kingdom of the Serbs, Croats, and Slovenes is formed.	1918		
The kingdom is renamed Yugoslavia.	1929	1929	Worldwide economic depression begins.
		1939	World War II begins, following the German invasion of Poland.
Serbia becomes one of the republics of the Socialist Federal Republic of Yugoslavia.	1945	1945	World War II ends.
Josip Broz Tito rules Yugoslavia.	1945–1980		
		1957	The Vietnam War starts.
		1969	Humans land on the moon.
		1975	The Vietnam War ends.
		1979	Soviet Union invades Afghanistan.
		1983	Drought and famine in Africa.
Slobodan Milošević, a Serbian nationalist, is elected president of Serbia.	1989	1989	The Berlin Wall is torn down, as communism crumbles in Eastern Europe.
Slovenia and Croatia declare their independence from Yugoslavia.	1991	1991	Soviet Union breaks into separate states.
Federal Republic of Yugoslavia is formed.	1992	1992	Bill Clinton is elected U.S. president.
Milosevic nullifies election results when the opposition wins; protests and demonstrations follow.	1996		
Milosevic is elected president of Yugoslavia.	1997		
Milosevic's repressive policies in Kosovo lead to international intervention; NATO bombs Serbia.	1999		
Vojislav Kostunica is elected president of Yugoslavia.	2000	2000	George W. Bush is elected U.S. president.
Zoran Djindjic becomes Serbia's prime minister.	2001	2001	Terrorists attack World Trade Center towers, New York, and Pentagon, Washington, D.C.
Yugoslavia is dissolved by Parliament, the new country is Serbia and Montenegro; Zoran Djindjic, Serbia's prime minister is assassinated. His replacement is to be determined.	2003		

Fast Facts

Official name: Republic of Serbia

Capital: Belgrade

Official language: Serbian

Belgrade

Serbia's flag

Stream near Peć

Official religion:	Serbian Orthodox Church
Year of founding:	Late 1100s
Founder:	Stefan Nemanja
Government:	Republic
Chief of state:	President
Head of government:	Prime minister
Area:	34,115 square miles (88,385 sq km)
Geographic center:	44° 00' N, 21° 00' E
Bordering countries:	Montenegro, Bosnia and Herzegovina, Croatia, Hungary, Romania, Bulgaria, Macedonia, Albania
Highest elevation:	Daravica, 8,714 feet (2,656 m)
Average temperatures:	70°F (21°C) in July; 32°F (0°C) in January
Average annual rainfall:	25–35 inches (64–89 cm)
National population (1997 est.):	10,500,000

Population of largest cities (1991 est.):

Belgrade (2002)	2,000,000
Novi Sad	179,626
Niš	175,391
Kragujevac	147,305
Priština	108,083
Subotica	100,386

Golubac Fortress

Famous landmarks:
- ▶ *Golubac Fortress*, Iron Gate Gorge
- ▶ *Kalemegdan Fortress*, Belgrade
- ▶ *Lepenski Vir* archaeological site, Djerdap National Park
- ▶ *Museum of Modern Art*, Belgrade
- ▶ *National Museum*, Belgrade
- ▶ *Turkish Baths and Sinan-pasha's Mosque*, Prizren
- ▶ *Historic monasteries and churches* are found all over Serbia, including Gracanica (Priština), Krušedol and Hopovo (Fruška Gora), the Patriarchate of Peć (Studenica and Zicak)
- ▶ *National parks:* Djerdap, Fruška Gora, Kopaonik, Mount Bolija, Sara, Tara

Industry: Food, textile, and metal processing; automobiles and agricultural machinery; household appliances; petroleum products; pharmaceuticals

Currency: One Yugoslav New Dinar (YUD) contains 100 paras. In 2002, the exchange rate was YD60 = $U.S.1

Weights and measures: Metric system

Literacy rate (1991 est.): Total population, 93%; males, 97.2%, females, 88.9%

Common Serbian words and phrases:

zdravo	hello
da	yes
ne	no
hvala	thank you
Razumem.	I understand.
Ne razumem.	I do not understand.

Currency

Schoolchildren

Nikola Tesla

Famous Serbs:

Ivo Andrić *Writer*	(1892–1975)
Stefan Dušan *King*	(1308–1388)
Mileva Marić Einstein *Scientist, first wife of Albert Einstein*	(1875–1948)
Draža Mihajlović *Soldier, resistance leader*	(1893–1946)
Slobodan Milošević *President*	(1941–)
Stefan Nemanja *Grand župan*	(d. 1200)
Stefan Nemanja *King*	(d. 1228)
Miloš Obrenović *Prince*	(1780–1860)
Mihajlo Pupin *Scientist, writer*	(1857–1935)
Saint Sava *Religious leader*	(c. 1176–c.1236)
Isidora Sekulić *Intellectual, writer*	(1877–1958)
Nikola Tesla *Electrical engineer, inventor*	(1856–1943)

To Find Out More

Nonfiction

▶ Andryszewski, Tricia. *Kosovo: The Splintering of Yugoslavia*. Brookfield, Conn.: Millbrook Press, 1998.

▶ Hunt, Inex, and Wantetta Draper. *Lightning in His Hand: Life Story of Nikola Tesla*. Thousand Oaks, Calif.: Sage Books, 1964.

▶ Kisslinger, Jerome. *The Serbian Americans*. New York: Chelsea House, 1990.

▶ *Little Falcons Magazine*. Edited by Father Thomas Kazich, published by the Serbian Orthodox Church, Grayslake, Ill.

▶ Pupin, Michael. *From Immigrant to Inventor*. 1924. Reprint, edited by I. Bernard Cohen. North Stratford, N.H.: Ayer, 1980.

▶ *Serb World USA Magazine*. Edited by Mary Nicklanovich Hart. Serb World USA, 415 E. Mabel Street, Tucson, AZ 85705

Web Sites

▶ **CIA World Factbook**
http://www.cia.gov/cia/publications/factbook/index.html
An overview of the geography, government, and economy of Yugoslavia

▶ **Facts about Serbia**
www.serbia.sr.gov.yu
Facts and information on the
government of Serbia, current events,
statistical data, and information on
the provinces and districts

▶ **National Tourism Organization**
of Serbia
www.serbia-info.com/ntos
Information on natural and cultural
tourist attractions in Serbia

▶ **Serbia: Royal History**
www.royalfamily.org/history/
index.htm
Information on the royal family
Nemanja, historic to the present day

▶ **B92**
http://www.b92.net
A popular independent radio station
offering news, music, art, video clips,
and live Internet radio via MP3 or
Real Player plug-ins

Organizations and Embassies

▶ **Embassy of Yugoslavia**
2134 Kalorama Road NW
Washington, DC 20008
(202) 332-0333

Index

Page numbers in *italics* indicate illustrations.

Meet the Author

JoAnn Milivojevic is a freelance writer and speaker who loves to travel and explore. During her youth, she traveled to Serbia several times and became fluent in the language. She returned to Serbia in 1998 to research the first edition of this book.

JoAnn has also written and lectured about the Caribbean. Her travel stories have appeared in magazines and newspapers nationwide, Fodor's Caribbean guidebook series, and a children's book on Puerto Rico. The first edition of *Serbia* was her first book for Children's Press.

JoAnn earned her B.A. in telecommunications from Indiana University and continued her education by pursuing a master's degree in creative writing. In 1980, she began her career in broadcasting. She eventually worked for several television stations as a writer/producer.

Today, she continues to produce select video projects and to write books, magazine articles, and interactive multimedia scripts for corporations. Her dog, Tolstoy, is her inspiration and constantly reminds her that roaming the great outdoors is as important to writing as tapping away on the keyboard.

Photo Credits